Basic Drawing for Games

Les Pardew

THOMSON

COURSE TECHNOLOGY

Professional ■ Technical ■ Reference

ISBN: 1-59200-951-4

Library of Congress Catalog Card Number: 2005929772

Printed in the United States of America

06 07 08 09 10 PA 10 9 8 7 6 5 4 3 2 1

THOMSON

COURSE TECHNOLOGY

Professional ■ Technical ■ Reference

Course PTR,
a division of Course Technology
25 Thomson Place
Boston, MA 02210
http://www.courseptr.com

Publisher and General Manager, Thomson Course Technology PTR:
Stacy L. Hiquet

Associate Director of Marketing:
Sarah O'Donnell

Manager of Editorial Services:
Heather Talbot

Marketing Manager:
Jordan Casey

Senior Acquisitions Editor:
Emi Smith

Senior Editor:
Mark Garvey

Project Editor:
Jenny Davidson

Thomson Course Technology PTR Editorial Services Coordinator:
Elizabeth Furbish

Interior Layout Tech:
Marian Hartsough

Cover Designer:
Mike Tanamachi

Indexer:
Sharon Hilgenberg

Proofreader:
Anne Smith

ACKNOWLEDGMENTS

I am grateful to a number of people whose assistance has helped me to write this book. I want to thank my family first because without the support of my wife Kim and my children, I would not be in a position to write a book. I am also grateful to all the great artists who went before me and showed me the way. They are the true pioneers in art and without their inspiration I would not have persevered to become an artist. I also want to thank the good people at Corel who support me with software and tools. In addition, I want to thank my editors and all the people at Thomson who are patient and kind to an artist as he tries to write a book. Thank you all.

About the Author

LES PARDEW was born and raised in Idaho. His hometown was a small farming community where he learned the benefits of hard work. His graduating high school class only numbered 33 individuals. From this small beginning, Pardew has grown to become a recognized leader in interactive entertainment.

Pardew is a video game and entertainment industry veteran, with over 20 years of industry experience. His artwork includes film and video production, magazine and book illustration, and more than 100 video game titles. He is the author or co-author of five books.

> *Game Art for Teens*
> *Beginning Illustration and Storyboarding*
> *Game Design for Teens*
> *Mastering Digital Art*
> *The Animator's Reference Book*

Pardew started his career in video games doing animation for *Magic Johnson Fast Break Basketball* for the Commodore 64. He went on to help create several major games including *Robin Hood: Prince of Thieves, Star Wars, Wrestle Mania, NCAA Basketball, Stanley Cup Hockey, Jack Nicholas Golf, Where in the World/USA Is Carman Sandiego, Starcraft Broodwars, Rainbow Six*, and *Cyber Tiger Woods Golf*, to name a few.

Pardew is an accomplished teacher having taught numerous art and business courses, including teaching as an adjunct faculty member at Brigham Young University's Marriott School of Management. He is also a business leader founding two separate game development studios and is a favorite speaker at video game conferences and events.

Les is the father of five wonderful children and the grandfather of one beautiful granddaughter. He loves being with his wife and children, serving in his church, and teaching art.

Contents

INTRODUCTION

This book is about drawing. Not drawing in general, although it will cover many basic drawing principles, but rather drawing as it relates to game development. It is a beginning book so it is written as if you have no previous experience in drawing for games. Each chapter will cover basic aspects of drawing as it relates to game development.

The first few chapters of the book will deal with basic drawing instruction to lay the foundation for you to progress toward good drawing. These chapters should be studied with care because they contain a lot of important information that will help you with the later chapters in the book.

The latter chapters in the book will be more specific to different aspects of drawing for games. They will cover things like environmental design, character design, storyboarding, and animation.

It is the goal of this book to help you become familiar with drawing for game development and to provide solid information on creating good drawings. It is just the beginning, however, and does not cover every aspect of drawing for games or drawing in general. It is my hope that reading and practicing the examples in this book will inspire you on your path to becoming a great game artist.

It all begins with drawing. Drawing is the foundation of art, and in many ways it is the most honest assessment of the artist's ability.

> *"Drawing is the honesty of art. There is no possibility of cheating. It is either good or bad."*
>
> —Salvador Dali

Learning to draw well will do more for you in opening a career in games than any other thing you can undertake.

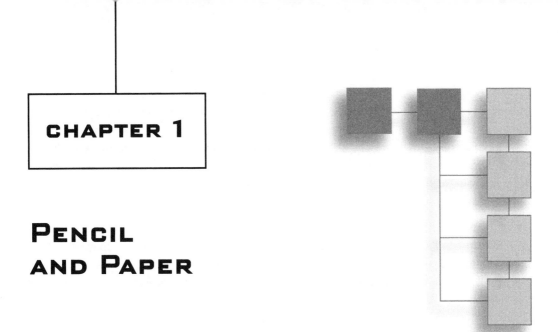

CHAPTER 1

PENCIL
AND PAPER

For the game artist it all starts with a pencil and a piece of paper. The ideas for the game have to be captured in a drawing before they can be realized in a game. The drawing may not actually appear in the game, but it will form the foundation for the artwork that eventually ends up in the game. It is important that game artists learn how to draw well. A game artist needs to draw with skill and imagination.

Understanding how to draw begins with understanding the tools of drawing. This chapter is an overview of tools used in drawing. Drawing with the wrong tools can be frustrating, causing the artist to be unable to achieve the desired effect for the finished picture. Drawing becomes much easier once you understand the tools.

The Pencil

Almost everyone knows what a pencil is. Pencils are made by the millions and sold in stores ranging from an art supply store to the corner convenience store. When you think of a pencil, you most likely think of a yellow object about seven inches long with an eraser at one end and a sharpened point at the other. Understanding where pencils came from and how a pencil is made will help you better select and use pencils for your artwork.

History of the Pencil

The exact origin of the pencil is unclear. The early Romans used metal styluses to mark papyrus. This may have been the earliest records kept using an instrument like what we think of as a pencil. These early tools would leave a mark on the papyrus but the mark was not very easy to read because it lacked contrast. The metals were usually too hard and the marks they made were gray rather than black.

It is believed that the first use of graphite was in England near Borrowdale in 1564. While uprooting a tree, some local shepherds noticed some black rocks in the roots of the tree. They found that the substance was brittle and soft and made dark black marks. It was probably first used to mark the sheep, but it didn't take long before the black rock was used for writing and drawing. They called the rocks "black lead." That may be why we use the word lead for the marking part of the pencil even though it is not lead at all but rather the substance we call graphite.

Using graphite without a holder was a messy business. Often the person would get more graphite on her hand than on the surface she wanted to mark. This fact spawned some ingenuity and experimentation with regard to developing holders for the graphite. Some early pencils were nothing more than graphite wrapped in string. Eventually the idea of encasing the graphite in wood became popular and the first pencils similar to what we use today were born.

Borrowdale graphite was the only known deposit of quality graphite. It was extremely valuable and only mined six weeks out of a year. Armed guards escorted the graphite to London. Exporting the graphite was illegal.

One problem with raw graphite is that it was brittle and broke easily. Another problem was that the graphite often had impurities that would cause it to scratch the drawing surface.

In 1795 a Frenchman by the name of Nicholas Jacques Conté developed a way of refining the graphite by grinding it and mixing it with finely ground clay. English graphite was very expensive so Conté was commissioned by an associate of Napoleon to create a writing instrument that didn't require the British graphite but was as good as the British pencils. Conté's mixture was extruded into thin lengths and fired to make the hard graphite sticks for the core of the pencil. This new process had many advantages.

The new pencils Conté made were much smoother to work with than the earlier pencils. The grinding process eliminated many of the impurities found in the raw graphite. Adding the clay also made it possible to vary the hardness of the graphite. Now artists could buy pencils with varying degrees of hardness. They could use hard graphite for drafting and clean light lines and softer graphite for bolder, darker lines and shading.

Conté's early pencils were simple devices. The graphite was extruded in long square-shaped lengths and fired. Then the graphite was placed in a small wooden rod with a trough cut into it so the graphite was in the middle, similar to today's pencils. A wooden v-shaped wedge was then pounded into the trough to hold the graphite in place.

As time passed, better milling methods were developed. Today graphite is processed in very much the same way that Conté developed but the lengths are usually round rather than square, and the graphite is glued into place between two pieces of wood. It you look at a wooden pencil where it has been sharpened, you can usually see a seam where the two pieces of wood are joined.

Some pencil manufacturers are starting to use plastic or other materials for encasing the graphite. I don't like these pencils because they tend to be pliable, meaning that they can be bent. I much prefer the wooden pencils because the wood grain is much stiffer and holds the pencil better without breaking.

Of course there are types of pencils other than wood. These are often called mechanical pencils. A mechanical pencil is really nothing more than a graphite holder. They are often similar to a pen in the way they look. The advantage of a mechanical pencil is that the holder can accept different types of graphite so the artist can use one pencil and still have a variety of softness of graphite.

Selecting a Pencil

The single most important aspect of selecting a pencil to draw with is the quality of the graphite. While most pencils will do an adequate job for writing a note or doing a quick sketch, they may not be suitable for more refined drawing. There are a number of characteristics that you should take into account when selecting a pencil.

- Graphite quality
- Graphite hardness
- Pencil size and shape

Graphite Quality

Cheap pencils often have inferior graphite, resulting in many more impurities. These impurities often are found as grit within the graphite causing the pencil to scratch the drawing surface.

Have you ever noticed while drawing that on occasion the pencil will seem to catch at the paper fibers and not draw as smoothly as before? That is because there is a small piece of grit in the graphite. This grit catches in the paper fibers and causes them to be lifted out of place. If you continue to draw with that pencil, the grit eventually will be released and become embedded in the paper fibers. Then as you continue to draw, the area around the piece of grit forms a small dark area, or hickey, in the drawing. This hickey can be very annoying when you are trying to create the effect of smooth, even shading. Figure 1.1 shows a piece of grit on a pencil.

Artist pencils tend to be more refined than common pencils, so the graphite has less grit. While a common pencil might be fine for sketching or line drawings, if you are doing any delicate drawing at all, a better quality pencil should be your choice.

Hard and Soft

The hardness of the graphite affects the amount of graphite that is transferred to the drawing surface during the drawing process. What really happens when you draw is that the graphite from the pencil is rubbed off the pencil and onto the paper. That is why you have to sharpen the pencil from time to time. Harder pencils have more clay mixed with the graphite than softer pencils. This means that less graphite is rubbed off during drawing—the result being a lighter line on the paper.

Pencils have a grading system to show how hard or soft the graphite is. In the US there are two basic systems: one using numbers alone and the other using numbers and letters (see Figure 1.2). There are, however, no standards among pencil manufactures, so a 4B pencil from one company may not exactly match a 4B pencil from another.

Figure 1.1 A small piece of grit in the graphite of the pencil will scratch the paper.

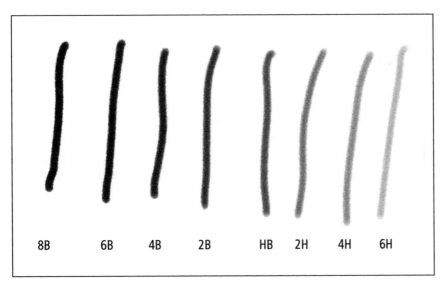

Figure 1.2 The softer the lead the darker the pencil mark.

For most drawing purposes, the softer pencils seem to work better than the harder pencils because they are more flexible in their use. With a soft pencil, the range of dark to light lines and shading can be controlled by the amount of pressure the artist applies when drawing. For example, when the artist needs very light construction lines, very light pressure is applied. When the artist needs darker shading and lines, more pressure is applied.

Harder pencils tend to require more pressure on the paper than softer pencils. The more pressure an artist uses on a drawing, the more likely there will be surface damage to the paper. When pressure is applied to paper from the pencil, the paper fibers are smashed together. Remember the old detective shows where the detective wants to read what the last message was on the note pad by the phone? Using a pencil he lightly shades over the page to reveal what was written before. The reason he can see a message there is because the person who wrote the message smashed the paper fibers when writing the note.

Smashed paper fibers is usually not a problem when someone is writing, but it can be a real problem when drawing. There is nothing more annoying than a crease appearing in the paper when you are trying to do some smooth shading on a drawing.

Shape and Size

Most pencils are similar in size and shape, but there are some important differences—the most important of which is the diameter of the graphite. If the graphite in a drawing pencil is large, then more of it will be exposed when the pencil is sharpened. However, if the pencil is sharpened to a point, what difference does the amount of exposed graphite make, you might be wondering? Well, if you only used the point to draw, it wouldn't make any difference. However, if you use the side of the pencil for shading, then it does make a difference. More exposed graphite means more graphite can come in contact with the paper during the shading process.

Another important aspect of a pencil is the shape of the graphite and the surrounding wood around the pencil. Some art pencils are not round but rather oval in their construction. The graphite in these pencils might be oval or even rectangular in shape. These pencils are often called sketching pencils. The advantage of the sketching pencil is that the graphite can be sharpened to a wedge rather than a point. A wedge is very useful when the artist wants to create uniform strokes on the paper. It is also useful when there needs to be some variation in the line. The artist can use a sketching pencil like a calligraphy pen to create thick and thin lines.

Most common pencils in the US have erasers attached to one end. Art pencils often don't have erasers. Artists tend to want to use art erasers rather than the common pink erasers because they are less abrasive to the paper. It is interesting to note that most pencils in Europe don't have erasers, probably because pencils in Europe have always come without erasers. The idea of putting an eraser on the end of the pencil is really an American idea.

Some pencils are round when looked at from an end while others are hexagonal in shape. This difference is minor and I have found very little difference between using one or the other.

Ebony

One of my favorite drawing pencils is called Ebony and is made by Faber Castle. The Ebony pencil has a high-quality graphite core that is large in diameter. The graphite is very smooth. I have found very little grit in the many Ebony pencils I have used over the years.

The graphite in the Ebony pencil strikes a nice balance between hard and soft. It is hard enough to achieve very dark blacks, while soft enough that it can do light work as well. Many of the drawings in this book were created using the Ebony pencil.

Paper

Like the pencil, paper is a very important part of drawing. Drawing is actually an abrasive process where the paper acts as the abrasive surface. When a pencil is rubbed against the surface of the paper, some of the graphite from the pencil is rubbed off. With this in mind, it is easy to see why the quality of the paper has a great deal to do with the quality of the drawing.

The more you understand about paper, the better you will be able to select and use the best paper for your drawing projects.

History of Paper

Paper as we know it today got its beginning in China around AD 105. T'sai Tzu, an aide to Emperor Ho-Ti of the Han dynasty, developed a process of creating a pulp from rags, old fishnets, and plant fiber. A screen passing through the pulp suspended in water caught individual fibers. The fibers on the screen were then dried to form thin sheets of paper.

Papermaking flourished in China for several years before it made its way to other Asian areas like Japan, Korea, Thailand, and Tibet. By AD 600, most of Asia had adopted the process of making paper. By 751 papermaking had spread to India where some Islamic warriors captured a caravan that included several Chinese papermakers. The warriors took the papermakers to Samarqand and thus established papermaking in the Islamic world.

Eventually papermaking spread to Baghdad, Damascus, Cairo, and Morocco. In AD 1100 the Moors brought papermaking to Spain and Portugal.

The Moors used reeds for their screens, and their process for creating pulp was not very refined. To make up for the imperfections, they coated their paper with a clay mixture so it would be a cleaner, more resilient surface for writing.

Papermaking spread to Italy where the Italians began to create paper, and from there it expanded into the rest of Europe. However, papermaking didn't become an industry until Gutenberg created the printing press and printed his famous bible in AD 1456.

Early paper was created primarily from old clothing. It was the use of rags to create paper that originated the term "rag" for designating paper made from cloth fibers like cotton. If a paper is made from 100% cotton it is marked 100% rag.

It wasn't until the 19th century that wood pulp was commonly used for making paper. Today vast tracks of forest are used in creating paper. The introduction of creating paper from wood was the turning point in making paper inexpensive.

Today paper is everywhere. It is so readily available that we often take it for granted and don't realize that it only became common for us to have paper in the last 200 years.

How Paper Is Made

Papermaking is a simple process, yet to make good drawing paper requires a certain amount of skill. Paper is made from fibers—usually cotton or wood fibers, but sometimes other fibers are used. The fibers are separated by a smashing process and suspended in liquid, usually water. The suspended fibers are called pulp.

A screen is then passed through the pulp solutions. As the screen passes through the pulp, the fibers collect on the screen in a thin sheet. The thickness of the paper is determined by the amount of fibers collected on the screen. When the collected fibers reach the desired thickness, the screen is removed from the pulp solution and the fibers are dried.

The texture of the paper is determined by how the fibers are dried and whether there are any additional smoothing processes. For example, if the fibers are allowed to dry on a drying screen, the finished paper will take on the texture of the screen. Figure 1.3 shows a close-up of a piece of paper with a screen pattern. This type of paper is often called a laid finish paper and is popular for documents like resumes or to be used as stationery.

Often paper will go through a pressing process to reduce the amount of surface texture. Very smooth papers are pressed using heated presses with high amounts of pressure. Using less heat and less pressure will result in a more uneven surface texture.

Some paper such as that used in magazines needs to be very smooth with almost no surface texture at all. It also needs to be nonabsorbent so that the ink will not bleed during the printing process. This paper is often coated with a very thin layer of clay. The clay fills in any texture in the paper fibers and acts as a barrier between the ink and the fibers. While this type of paper might be good for pen ink drawings, it is not very good for pencil drawings because a pencil needs texture on the paper surface to catch the graphite.

Figure 1.3 The laid finish comes from the pattern of the drying screen.

Selecting Paper

The paper you use should be selected based on the type of drawing you intend to create. If you are creating a highly finished smooth shaded drawing, the texture of the paper should be very smooth. On the other hand, if your drawing takes advantage of the texture of the paper, you will want to select a paper that has more of a texture so the texture of the paper shows through in the drawing.

Figure 1.4 shows several different papers with differing textures. Notice that some of the papers have a mechanical pattern while others seem to have a more natural and random texture.

Fibers

Paper is made up of many small thread-like fibers intertwined together. The most common fiber used in paper is cellulose made from wood pulp. Wood fibers tend to be short and thus create a more brittle paper. Cotton fibers are longer and more flexible than wood fibers. Cotton is also naturally acid free. Most of the better quality art papers are made from cotton. Wood-fiber paper is getting better but is still considered inferior by most artists.

Figure 1.4 Textures differ from paper to paper.

Surface

There are several types of paper surfaces, including hot press, plate, coated, vellum, cold press, rough, and tracing.

Hot Press

Hot press paper is paper that is pressed by hot rollers to create a smooth, hard surface. Hot pressed paper is good for fine drawing but may be too smooth for some drawings. Many artists like the smooth texture of hot pressed paper because there are seldom irregularities in the paper and it is easier to create smooth shading effects.

Plate

Plate is a process of pressing paper tightly with a smooth metal plate to create a very smooth, very hard surface. Plate paper is usually not a good choice for drawing paper because it has little texture to grab the graphite.

Coated

Coated paper is paper that is coated with a thin layer of some nonabsorbent material like clay. Coated paper is most often used in printing, where the coating keeps the ink from being absorbed by the paper fibers and spreading. Coated paper usually has a shiny surface that is difficult to draw on.

Vellum

A vellum surface is a good surface for drawing. The word vellum comes from the ancient process of making writing surfaces from the stretched skins of animals. Vellum was the primary writing and drawing surface in Europe prior to the introduction of paper. In describing a surface, the word vellum refers to a surface that is similar to the vellum used in ancient times. It has enough texture to hold a pencil line but not so much texture as to interfere with fine shading. The texture is often small so that unwanted patterns don't appear in the drawing.

Cold Press

Cold press is paper that is pressed with cold rollers. It is generally rougher than vellum or hot press paper and has a very obvious texture. It is a good drawing paper for sketching and bolder pencil work, but often the texture is too pronounced for fine shading.

Rough

Rough paper is most often used by watercolor artists. It has a rough, uneven texture that can create interesting patterns when used for drawings. These patterns become a problem, however, if a smoother shaded finish is desired.

Tracing

Tracing paper is a very smooth translucent paper used for tracing. It is used by artists when there is a need to transfer all or part of a drawing from one sheet to another like in animation. Tracing paper has a vellum finish and is sometimes referred to as tracing vellum.

Thickness

The thickness of the paper is also an important consideration when choosing a drawing surface. Thicker paper tends to be stronger than thinner paper because there are more interlocking paper fibers. Thicker paper also has more resistance to pencil pressure, which will reduce the amount of indentations from one page to the next when you are drawing in a pad of paper.

Paper thickness is measured in weight per ream in the US. A ream is 500 sheets of paper. For example, if 500 sheets of paper weighed 200 pounds, then the paper would be labeled 200 lb paper. The drawback to this kind of measuring system is that not all paper is the same size, so a 200 lb paper from one company may not be the same as a 200 lb paper from another.

Acid

Acid content in paper will cause the paper to turn yellow and become brittle over time. Most of the better drawing paper is acid free, which means that there is either no acid in the fibers or that buffers have been added to the paper to offset the acid content. Paper made from cotton is naturally acid free. Make sure that you choose an acid-free paper when you are doing a finished drawing. Some drawing paper, like newsprint paper, is not acid free. Newsprint paper is inexpensive paper used for sketching. It is not generally used for finished drawings.

Tooth

Tooth is a word many artists use to describe the abrasive qualities of a paper. A paper's tooth refers to how much graphite the paper will scrub off from the pencil. Some papers will have little tooth, causing the graphite to appear light on the paper, while other paper may have a great deal of tooth, causing the graphite to come off the pencil faster.

More than anything tooth is a matter of comfort for the artist. Some artists like a lot of tooth in their paper and some like little. If you like to create delicate drawings, selecting a paper with little tooth may be your best choice. If you like to be bold and direct in your drawings greater tooth might be a better choice.

Color

Some drawing paper is colored. Colored paper is not generally used for pencil drawings. It is more commonly used for charcoal or pastel drawings where there is both darker and lighter media than the color of the paper. Using colored paper for a pencil drawing will limit the amount of light to dark contrast in the picture because the lightest part of the drawing will be the paper.

Testing Papers

If you can test a few papers before you choose one to draw on you will have a much better idea of how the paper will react to the pencil. Sometimes art supply stores will have small sample squares of paper that you can test right in the store. To test the paper take a soft pencil, 2B or softer, and lightly scrub the side of the graphite across the paper. The softer the graphite in the pencil, the easier it will be to see the pattern and texture of the paper. Notice the pattern of the paper's texture and how well the paper takes the graphite. A good drawing paper will receive the graphite in a smooth even manner and it will be easy to blend your strokes. Poor drawing papers will make it more difficult to blend strokes.

Erasers

I mention erasers last because while they may be necessary, they should be used sparingly. Erasing can cause paper damage, so the less you need to erase your picture the better.

Erasers come in many different shapes and types, most of which are not good for use on delicate drawing paper. The less abrasive the eraser, the better it will be to use on your drawings. Never ever use the eraser that comes on the end of a pencil. Most of the time these erasers are cheap and tend to not only be highly abrasive, but they also will on occasion smear the picture rather than clean it. This is especially true of some of the cheaper pencils.

The eraser most commonly used by artists is a kneaded eraser. The name kneaded comes from the fact that the eraser is malleable like bread dough. Being malleable, the eraser can be shaped into almost any shape imaginable from a sharp point for detailed touchups to a broad wedge for large clean-ups.

Kneaded erasers are usually much less abrasive than other erasers. The better ones will have a fine even texture. Some of the cheaper ones will feel gritty.

All erasers leave a residue on the paper. A kneaded eraser leaves very fine particles almost like sand. Other types of erasers will often leave large particles on the paper. To remove the residue the artist will need to brush the drawing very lightly with a finger or soft brush. Sometimes blowing on the paper will remove most of the residues but usually not all of them. You should be very careful when removing residue so that you don't smear any of your drawing.

Computers

Not all drawing is done with a pencil and paper. Many artists in the game industry use a computer as their drawing tool. Using a computer has many advantages and also some disadvantages. Some of the advantages include the elimination of surface problems, flexibility of tools, and a cool feature called undo. Some of the disadvantages include cost, no direct feel of the surface, and limitations of the stylus.

When you use a computer, there is no actual drawing surface so there is no chance that you will mess up the surface by erasing too much. Some drawing software simulates different paper textures. A fun feature of simulated textures is that changes can be made to the surface texture while drawing. This means that if you want a heavy texture for one area of your drawing and a smooth texture for another area, you can change the texture for drawing in one area and then change it back when drawing in another.

Computer drawing programs are very sophisticated and flexible. They contain a number of tools and features that make it possible to gain almost any drawing effect imaginable, including adding text, creating shadows, and adding special effects.

One of the best aspects of drawing on a computer is the undo feature. Undo eliminates the last drawing action. This means that you can experiment with your drawing and if you don't like it you can use the undo feature to return the drawing back to where you started. Some drawing software allows for multiple undos, meaning that you can back out of multiple drawing steps if you don't like them.

Drawing on the computer takes specialized software and hardware, which can be expensive. Software programs can cost hundreds of dollars for the better ones. Hardware costs can run even more depending on the type of system.

While drawing on the computer may eliminate surface problems, it eliminates the surface too. For artists who draw by feel as much as sight, the missing surface can be a problem. Many artists enjoy the feel of the pencil on the surface as they draw.

The stylus used for most drawing applications is a pressure-sensitive device that looks like a ballpoint pen. This type of device is good for drawing lines and strokes but it is not well-suited to fine shading like a normal pencil. You can't lay a stylus on its side to do fine shading like you can a normal pencil.

Software

There are two basic types of drawing programs: raster, or bitmap, and vector.

Raster, or bitmap, programs are image creation programs that use small dots called pixels to create images. Each pixel can change in value, light to dark, and color. Vector programs are programs that create editable lines using mathematical vector technology.

Bitmap Art Programs

The most common software used for drawing in the game industry is Adobe Photoshop. Photoshop is a very sophisticated 2D graphics program that is used for almost any 2D purpose in the game studio. It has a wide range of features and functions from delicate photo retouching to special effects. Photoshop has specialized brushes that can simulate pencils. Figure 1.5 shows a screenshot of Photoshop.

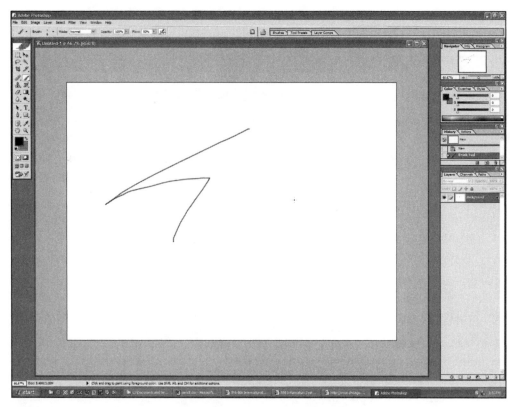

Figure 1.5 Photoshop is a good choice for creating art on the computer.

One of the best software programs for drawing is Corel Painter. Painter simulates natural media, meaning that using the program is similar to working with paints or graphite or other media. In Painter, for example, you can paint with an airbrush or you can paint with oils. It also simulates chalk, markers, watercolor, and of course a pencil. In fact, Painter has several different types of pencils to choose from, including a 2B pencil. Figure 1.6 shows a screenshot of Painter with a pencil selected.

Painter has several different styles of pencils and papers. It simulates the drawing process so that the drawing seems natural. Drawings created in Painter are difficult to distinguish from drawings on paper. Figure 1.7 shows a drawing created in Painter.

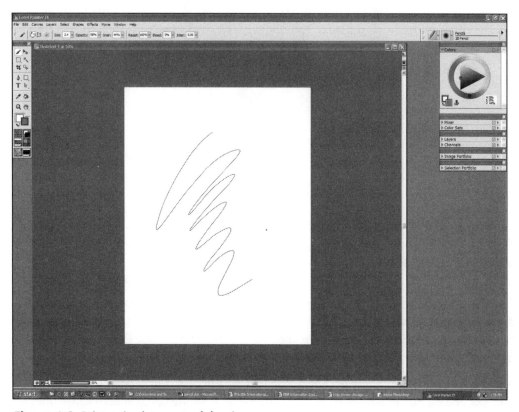

Figure 1.6 Painter simulates natural drawing.

Figure 1.7 This drawing was created in Painter.

Vector Drawing Programs

Vector drawing programs approach the drawing process from a very different perspective. These programs use vectors to create the lines of the drawings. Vectors are mathematical representations of lines in the program. Because the lines are converted into vectors, they can be edited after drawing. Figure 1.8 shows a screenshot of Adobe Illustrator, one of the most popular vector drawing programs.

Notice in the figure that there is a sharp curve in the line. This curve was changed after the line was drawn. Editable lines are great for drawing. Imagine being able to move lines on your paper until you have them just right.

The problem with vector drawing programs is that they are not as close to the natural drawing process as bitmap programs. The drawing process is similar, but from then on everything is different. The lines can be moved. The line is separate from the drawing surface. There is little if any support for fine shading or other pencil-like functions.

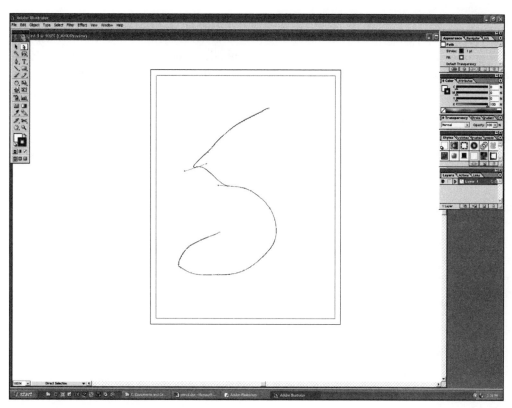

Figure 1.8 Lines in vector programs can be edited.

Hardware

Most computers don't come equipped with specialized hardware for drawing. They come with a mouse and a keyboard. The mouse can be used for drawing, but it is a clumsy instrument and not well-suited to delicate work. Trying to draw with a keyboard is next to impossible. When I first started creating art for games, I had to use a keyboard to create the art, a frustrating process at best.

A digitizing tablet and stylus are much easier to use for drawing than a mouse. A digitizing tablet is a slate like peripheral with a flat surface. A stylus that looks similar to a ball-point pen is used over the tablet. The stylus has a pressure-sensitive tip that allows the artist to vary the pressure of a stroke similar to drawing with a real pencil. When greater pressure is applied to the tablet through the stylus, it usually translates into a darker or bolder mark in the drawing.

The main advantage of using a digitizing tablet is that you can hold the stylus similar to how you hold a pencil. Many styluses have pressure-sensitive points on both ends. The smaller one acts as a writing or drawing device while the larger one acts as an eraser. Some will have buttons along the side that can be used in the same way that a mouse button is used.

Some digitizing surfaces are attached directly to the screen of a flat panel monitor. These devices, while expensive, are a great improvement, allowing the artist to draw directly to the drawing. No longer does the computer artist have to look at the screen while drawing somewhere else. Now drawing can be performed directly on the screen.

Summary

Wow, we have covered a lot in this chapter. Not only did the chapter contain information on the history of drawing materials, it also offered suggestions on how to select the right materials for different types of drawings. In this chapter the following topics were covered:

- History of the pencil
- Types of pencils
- Selecting a good drawing pencil
- History of paper
- How paper is made
- Selecting paper
- Erasers
- Drawing on the computer

All of this information may seem a little dull when you want to jump right in and start drawing, but it is very important to select the right tools and materials for drawing. Inferior tools and materials will result in amateurish-looking drawings.

Questions

1. What is the dark marking material used in pencils?
2. Conté mixed what two ingredients together to create his pencils?
3. How is the hardness of graphite varied in pencil making?
4. What type of pencil is softer, a 2B pencil or a 2H pencil?
5. Impurities in a pencil can cause what problem while drawing?
6. Where is it believed that the first paper was created?
7. What cloth-like material was used in the early days of papermaking in Europe?
8. Why is a vellum surface better than a plate surface for most drawing?

9. Why is coated paper not often used for pencil drawings?

10. Why is it better to use a soft pencil rather than a hard pencil when testing paper?

11. What damage can result from erasing a drawing?

12. What type of eraser can be molded into any shape and is commonly used by most artists?

13. Are computers used by artists in the game industry for drawing?

14. Which type of drawing program is most like natural drawing, vector or bitmap?

15. What is a digitizing tablet?

Answers

1. Graphite

2. Graphite and clay

3. The ratio of clay to graphite

4. 2B

5. Scratching the drawing surface

6. China

7. Rags

8. It has more tooth

9. It has little or no tooth

10. It is easier to see the texture patterns

11. Damage to the paper fibers

12. A kneaded eraser

13. Yes

14. Bitmap

15. A device used by a computer artist to draw

Discussion Questions

1. What should an artist think about when choosing the hardness of the pencil for a drawing?

2. Why do most artists prefer softer pencils for drawing?

3. Why is cotton a better material for making paper than wood?

4. Explain why very rough or very smooth paper may not be the best choice for drawing.

5. Explain what advantages drawing on a computer has over drawing with a pencil and paper.

Exercises

1. Create a small drawing using a hard pencil and another using a soft pencil. Explain the advantages and problems with each.

2. Find samples of several different types of paper. Test each type of paper for drawing and list its advantages and disadvantages.

3. Draw a simple drawing using a computer.

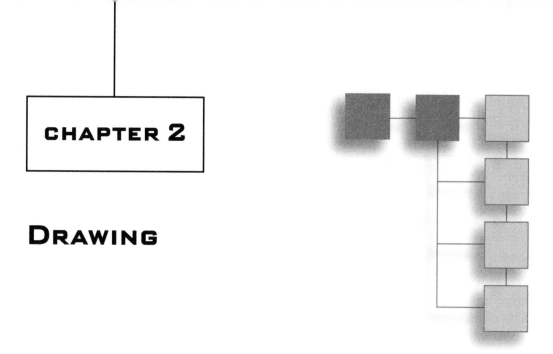

CHAPTER 2

DRAWING

Drawing is the process of interpreting the artist's vision into a two-dimensional representation. A good drawing requires two separate major elements:

- The artist needs to have a compelling vision.
- The artist needs to have the drawing skills to express the compelling vision.

This chapter and most of this book will be devoted to helping you gain the skills you need to express your vision. While some time will be given to achieving a compelling vision, vision is something that is personal for each artist.

Skill in Drawing

In some ways drawing is a performing art similar to playing a musical instrument. It requires skill in execution. Like a musician who has to understand how to hold and use a bow on a violin, the artist has to understand how to hold and use a pencil. Drawing skill can be broken down into two major groups: method and knowledge.

Drawing method encompasses all uses of the pencil on paper to create a drawing, including how to hold the pencil, pencil strokes on the paper, shading techniques, and drawing style.

Drawing knowledge encompasses things like perspective design and understanding of the subject. For example, an artist must understand basic anatomy in order to have the ability to draw a person with any degree of accuracy.

Holding and Using the Pencil

One of the biggest problems beginning artists have is that they don't hold the pencil correctly for drawing. The problem is not so much that the artist holds the pencil wrong as it is that the artist needs to learn how to hold the pencil in different ways for different purposes. Most beginning artists will hold the pencil for drawing the same way they hold it for writing.

Drawing is a very different process from writing. When a person writes, he is creating precise small characters on a paper. While this action is similar to drawing where precise detail is needed, it is very different from the action needed for blocking in a drawing or for achieving fine, smooth shading.

When a pencil is held in the writing position, beginning artists tend to tighten up and limit the movement of the pencil to the range of motion in the fingers. This is because the hand rests on the paper. Figure 2.1 shows the typical writing position of the hand.

In the initial stages of a drawing, freedom of movement is very important. Try holding the pencil similar to how you would hold a butter knife. Figure 2.2 shows how the pencil should be held.

Holding the pencil in the butter knife position makes it almost impossible to draw with only finger movement. Instead, the whole arm is brought into play. If this is the first time you have ever drawn holding a pencil in the butter knife position, it may feel a little awkward at first. Stay with it until you become comfortable. The long-term benefits from learning to hold your pencil in this position are immeasurable. It will allow you to draw with much more freedom than the writing position.

Figure 2.1 When writing, the palm of the hand rests on the paper.

Figure 2.2 Hold the pencil like a butter knife.

Let's do a little practicing. Find yourself some paper and a pencil. The paper should be large because I want you to have to move your arm. The pencil should be a soft pencil so that it will be easy for you to see your drawing. I recommend using newsprint for the paper and at least a 2B or softer pencil.

Figure 2.3 is a picture taken from my book *The Animator's Reference Book* published by Thompson Course Technology. This book is a great source for artistic reference of the human body in a variety of actions. We will use it here to help you loosen the way you start a drawing.

Prop your drawing surface up so that it is almost parallel with your own torso. This will make it easier to draw with the pencil in the butter knife position. Now quickly sketch the photo. Try to capture the essence of the feeling of movement in less than 60 seconds. Yes, this is speed drawing and it is good for you, so don't complain about the time limit. You're not doing a finished drawing. This is just an exercise. It's kind of like

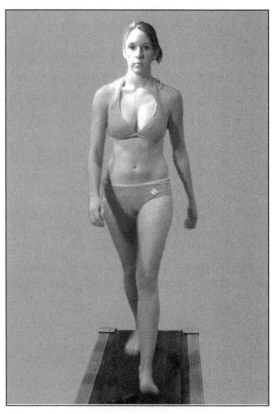

Figure 2.3 Draw this figure quickly and loosely.

stretching before a long-distance race. You need to get loosened up.

Figure 2.4 is a sketch of Figure 2.3. Your sketch should be similar, but it is okay if it is not exactly the same. I made this sketch in about 30 seconds focusing only on trying to capture the feeling of movement. There probably isn't a single line in the drawing that is technically accurate with regard to the exact outline of the figure. In fact, most of the lines in this drawing follow the skeleton of the figure more than they do the outside shape.

In order for you to draw with the pencil in the butter knife position you have to move your arm, not your fingers. The human body is an organic yet mechanical mechanism. The muscles in our arms are like hydraulic pistons contracting and expanding to create movement. Unlike hydraulics, however, the placement of the muscles and the way they are

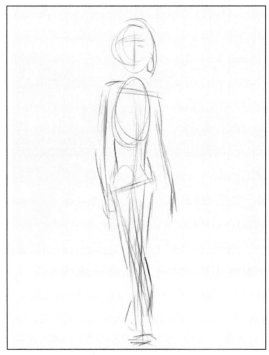

Figure 2.4 Imagine the skeleton of the figure when drawing.

attached to the bones of our skeleton is very organic. This is very important because it allows the body to move in fluid, nonmechanical ways. It is the attachment of the muscles and the shape of our bones that allow for grace of movement. Why is all of this important? Because in many ways the artist needs to learn how to dance with the drawing.

Dancing with the Drawing

Dancing with the drawing means that the artist takes advantage of the natural motions of his body to add expression to the drawings. By holding the pencil in the butter knife position, the artist is better able to dance with the drawing. In other words, think of yourself as a dancer. Try to move your arm in graceful, smooth, flowing motions. It isn't that you are giving up control of your drawing; rather, it is that you are gaining control by letting the natural rhythm of your body express itself in your drawings.

Now try a couple more drawings. Figures 2.5 and 2.6 are two more photographs from *The Animator's Reference Book*. Use them for a study and quickly sketch both pictures. Try to indicate as quickly as you can the basic motion captured in the photo. If you need to, draw them several times until you feel good about your creation. The idea here is not to create an accurate picture, but rather to indicate the essence of the figure.

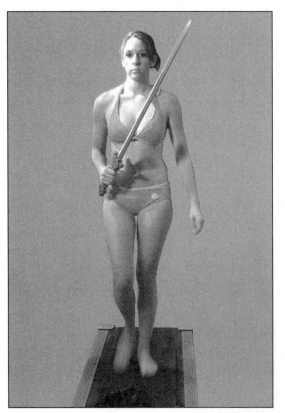

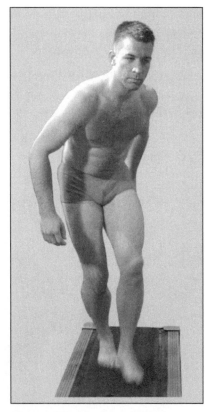

Figure 2.5 The figure is walking while holding a sword.

Figure 2.6 The figure is leaning forward while walking.

Hint

As you draw, you will hopefully notice that there is a main line of motion in each figure. The main line of motion is the foundation line of capturing the motion of the figure. To find the main line of motion, create a line from the head following the spine down through the leg that is holding most of the weight of the body. Try drawing this line first and then attaching the rest of the body to this line. It will help you gain a feeling for motion.

The butter knife position is great for starting a drawing, but it doesn't work too well for fine detail of delicate shading. The writing position is better for fine detail, but you will need to learn another way to hold the pencil for delicate shading.

Balancing the Pencil

The best way to achieve delicate, smooth gradations in shading over larger areas on your drawing is to lightly stroke the side of the graphite against the paper. The butter knife position and the writing position don't work well for light strokes. A better way to hold your pencil is to balance it between the finger and the thumb, as shown in Figure 2.7. We will call this the balanced position.

In the balanced position, the thumb and the finger act as a hinge. The little finger is then used to gently apply pressure, giving you great control over the amount of graphite that is applied to the drawing with each stroke.

Try using the balanced pencil position to gently shade a large area from light to dark, as shown in Figure 2.8.

Figure 2.7 Balance the pencil between the thumb and the finger.

Figure 2.8 Use the balanced pencil position to smoothly shade an area.

With a little practice, you should gain very fine control over shading your drawings. Try shading from light to dark and from dark to light with a variety of shapes. As you shade, attempt to keep the shaded areas smooth and clean.

Be Good to Your Paper

Be good to your paper and your paper will be good to you. Paper fibers are delicate and become damaged very easily. Harsh drawing and excessive erasing destroy the surface quality of the paper. Once the paper is damaged, it can't be repaired.

Damaged paper creates an uneven drawing surface. The damaged area will receive the graphite differently than the undamaged areas. If the paper fibers are raised by the abrasive use of an eraser, the damaged area will have more tooth than the surrounding paper. It is almost impossible to compensate for damaged areas when doing delicate pencil work.

A common mistake of beginning artists is to use the eraser too frequently. Experienced artists tend to rarely ever erase. If you must erase an area, the best eraser to use is a kneaded eraser as mentioned in Chapter 1. Kneaded erasers are less abrasive than other erasers, and they leave fewer residues behind. They also can be molded to any shape—a useful trait when you want to do fine touchup work on your drawing. See Figure 2.9.

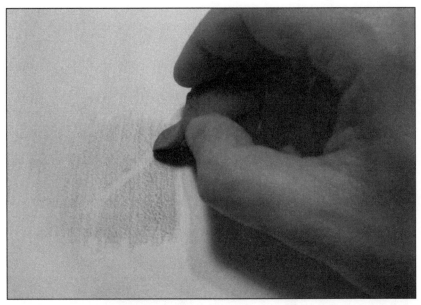

Figure 2.9 A kneaded eraser can be used to touch up fine detail in a drawing.

Your hand can also cause problems with the drawing surface. The pores in the skin of the hand secrete oil. The oil is used by the body to keep our skin soft. Without the oil, the skin of our hands would be rough and tend to crack. Though this oil is good for our hands, it is not good for drawing paper. The oil from your hand can cause slick spots on the paper that won't receive graphite as well as the rest of the paper.

The best way to avoid oil from your hand getting on your paper is to use a barrier piece of paper between your hand and the drawing surface. Figure 2.10 shows a barrier sheet of paper used in drawing.

The barrier paper serves two purposes. The first is to keep oil from your hand from getting on the paper. The second is that it helps to prevent smearing. I often see work from beginning and sometimes even advanced artists with smears and smudges on it.

Pencil Strokes

Drawings are made up of pencil strokes. Pencil strokes can be bold, light, flowing, or smooth. They affect both the look and feel of a drawing. The type of pencil strokes an artist uses to create a drawing is a personal choice and is as individual as a person's handwriting. Beginning artists should explore different ways of drawing until they are comfortable with a drawing technique.

Figure 2.10 Place a sheet of paper between your hand and the drawing.

Figure 2.11 shows a simple zigzag stroke. This stroke is one of the quickest ways to shade an area. The drawback of a stroke like this is that while it tends to work well for shading flat areas, it does not express much about the nature of the surface. A zigzag stroke is often used in quick sketches like thumbnails or storyboards. Another problem with the zigzag stroke is that the ends of the stroke are darker than the middle.

Figure 2.12 shows a stroke that is similar to the zigzag stroke but is created with a

Figure 2.11 A zigzag stroke is one of the quickest ways to shade an area.

Figure 2.12 A scrubbing motion can create a smooth gradation.

more circular scrubbing motion. The stroke is a buildup stroke where the side of the graphite is lightly rubbed over the paper, building up the darker tones over time. This stroke is used for fine, smooth gradations in drawings. It is not an expressive stroke, but rather a stroke used for smooth shading. When using this method, the artist is attempting to hide any evidence of the individual pencil strokes.

Figure 2.13 Directional strokes are separate lines drawn next to each other.

Figure 2.13 shows a directional stroke. Each stroke is a separate line drawn with the pencil. Directional strokes can be used for shading just like zigzag strokes, but they can be more expressive because they can follow the direction of the shape. Directional strokes also don't have the disadvantage of being darker at the ends like the zigzag stroke.

A variation on the directional stroke is a weighted directional stroke. In it the artist applies more pressure to one end of the stroke than the other. Figure 2.14 shows a weighted directional stroke used to draw a lock of hair.

Figure 2.14 A lock of hair can be drawn using a weighted directional stroke.

By changing the direction of the pencil strokes, the artist can create a shading method called crosshatching. Crosshatching is a method of using directional strokes that overlap from different directions to create textures or shading. Crosshatching is often used in pen and ink drawings. Figure 2.15 shows some stone brick rendered with a crosshatch stroke.

Sometimes the artist can use pencil strokes to describe an object. In Figure 2.16 pencil strokes are used to create a pine tree, a branch of leaves, and some grass around a rock.

Figure 2.15 Crosshatching is another method of pencil shading.

Figure 2.16 Pencil strokes can be used to describe an object.

These are just a few types of strokes that an artist can use in drawing. There are as many variations as you can imagine.

Shading Techniques

Shading is the process of using pencil strokes to create areas of value from light to dark. It is used to show light and shadow on objects or other changes in value like a dark color next to a light one.

When drawing with a pencil on a white sheet of paper, the white of the paper acts as the lightest areas. The values go then from the light of the paper to the darkest area of the drawing. The variation from light to dark in a drawing can be smooth or abrupt, depending on the subject and style of the artist.

Shading in a drawing is generally used to add volume and definition to a drawing. In the case of a portrait like Figure 2.17 the face is shaded using very gentle strokes to give it a smooth subtle variation in value. The hair, on the other hand, received stronger, more direct strokes to help define the direction of the strands. The eyes have very abrupt changes in value.

Some drawings seek to eliminate all evidence of any lines. These drawings are called value drawings, and they can approach the detail and clarity of black and white photography.

Shading is usually one of the last steps an artist will take in completing a drawing. When drawing, the artist will generally rough in the idea using mostly lines with very little shading. Figure 2.18 shows an idea roughed in lightly.

Figure 2.17 Shading can be used to add volume and define detail in a picture.

Figure 2.18 Shading is not used in the early stages of drawing.

Once a picture is roughed in and the artist is comfortable with the composition, it is a good idea to create a value sketch. A value sketch is a small thumbnail sketch that defines the light and dark areas of a picture without much detail. It is usually better to create the sketch small so the temptation to overwork the detail is minimized. Figure 2.19 shows the value sketch for this picture.

From the values defined in the value sketch, the finished sketch is then shaded. Figure 2.20 shows the shading applied to the sketch. Notice how much stronger the images of the picture are with the shading added.

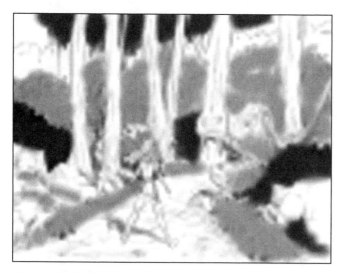

Figure 2.19 Make a value sketch before adding the shading to a picture.

Figure 2.20 The finished drawing with shading.

Shading usually takes some time, so defining the areas in a small sketch helps to solve many of the design issues before the artist commits to the time it will take to finish the drawing.

Drawing Knowledge

Good drawing has a lot to do with how much the artist knows. Artists often study their preferred subject matter for years to learn as much as they can about drawing that subject. Artists tend to need to know a lot about the world around them if they want to be proficient in depicting that world in their work. This becomes even more important in drawing for games because often drawings for games come from the artist's imagination. For example, knowledge of light is essential to understanding light and shadow on objects in a drawing. Anatomy is essential to the artist who wants to draw the human figure. Knowledge of clothing and how it reacts to form and gravity is important in understanding how to construct costumes for game characters.

This book could never cover all of the knowledge that a person might need in a career of drawing for games. Only the basics like perspective and composition will be covered here. After you have mastered the concepts in this book, you can then continue your study in whatever specialized subjects you find interesting.

Perspective

Perspective is the representation of objects or characters in a picture so that they appear to relate to each other on the paper as they would in nature. In the natural world items appear smaller the farther away they are from the viewer. For example, if someone is standing next to the viewer, he will appear larger. If that person were to walk away from the viewer, he would appear to recede in size. When an artist draws a scene, objects and characters need to be sized so that they are correct in relation to other objects or characters in the scene.

Linear Perspective

One of the most common ways for an artist to correctly establish the sizes of objects in a scene is to use linear perspective. Linear perspective is the process of using lines drawn from a vanishing point on the horizon to correctly size the objects or characters in a drawing. To understand how perspective works, the artist needs to understand the concept of having a horizon line.

Horizon Line

A horizon line is the line where the ground meets the sky. In Figure 2.21, the darker gray area on the bottom represents the ground; the lighter gray on the top represents the sky. The black line where the two meet is the horizon line.

The horizon line will form the basis for linear perspective. It changes depending on the angle that is used in the picture. For example, viewing a plane in the air will lower the horizon line as shown in Figure 2.22.

Figure 2.21 The line between the ground and the sky is the horizon line.

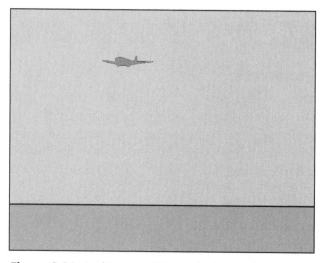

Figure 2.22 Looking up will lower the horizon line.

On the other hand, viewing a boat from a hillside will move the horizon line up as shown in Figure 2.23.

Sometimes objects in the scene like mountains or buildings will obscure the horizon line. In these instances the artist has to determine where the horizon line is based on the view and the slope of the ground. In Figure 2.24, the horizon line is estimated because the buildings are blocking a clear view of the horizon.

Figure 2.23 Looking down will raise the horizon line.

Figure 2.24 The artist sometimes needs to estimate the horizon line.

Vanishing Point

Another concept that is important to linear perspective is the vanishing point. A vanishing point is a point on the horizon that an object or character recedes to. A good example is to imagine standing in the middle of a straight road. The point at which the road meets the sky is the vanishing point. Figure 2.25 shows this concept.

The vanishing point can be used to determine the relative size of any object in the picture. In Figure 2.26 two lines drawn from the vanishing point are used as a guide for how large the character should be.

In this example only one vanishing point is used. This is termed *single-point perspective* because all the objects in the picture are receding to a single vanishing point. Single-point linear perspective is the most basic form of linear perspective.

The most common type of linear perspective is two-point perspective. In two-point perspective, objects are defined by two separate vanishing points. Figure 2.27 shows an example of two-point perspective.

Two-point perspective adds to the realism of a picture because it allows for more planes on the object to recede from view. Look at the difference between the cube in Figure 2.26 and the two cubes in Figure 2.27. In Figure 2.26 there is no way to plot the plane facing us with one vanishing point. This is okay if the plane facing the viewer is perpendicular to the viewer, but it presents problems if there is even a slight rotation of view. With two-point perspective, the additional vanishing point makes it possible for the artist to draw an object from any angle.

Figure 2.25 The vanishing point is where the road meets the sky.

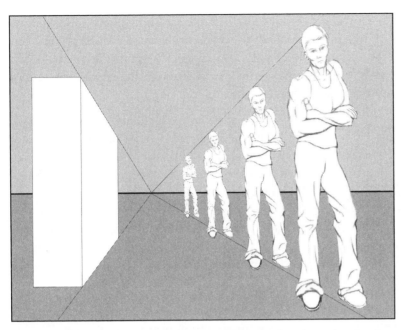

Figure 2.26 Lines from the vanishing point are used to determine the size of the character.

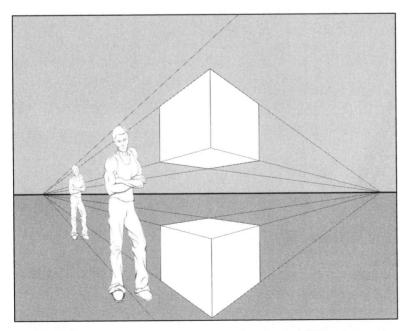

Figure 2.27 Two-point linear perspective uses two vanishing points to plot objects.

All objects in a picture are not always oriented to the same vanishing points. If the picture is of a city street, the buildings may line up with a similar or the same vanishing point, but other objects in the scene will most likely not. By changing the vanishing points for the objects in a scene, the artist is able to change their orientation to the viewer. Figure 2.28 shows several cubes with different vanishing points.

Two-point perspective will be adequate for the artist in most situations, but some will require even more accuracy. Notice that in two-point perspective, all of the vertical lines are parallel with each other. This isn't very noticeable to us because often the convergences of these lines are so distant that most of the time we don't notice the difference. Some objects are so massive that they will look odd with only two-point perspective. In addition, extreme camera angles often call for more than a two-point approach. That is where three-point linear perspective comes into play. With the addition of a third point not connected with the horizon line, the artist is able to have the object recede from view correctly. Figure 2.29 shows how three-point perspective works. The cubes seem more massive with the addition of a third point.

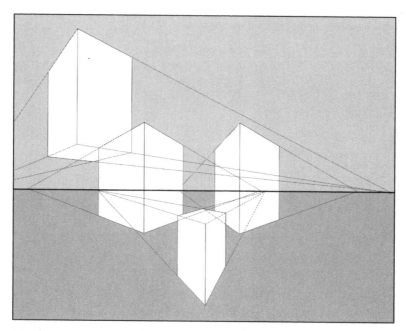

Figure 2.28 Most objects have their own vanishing points.

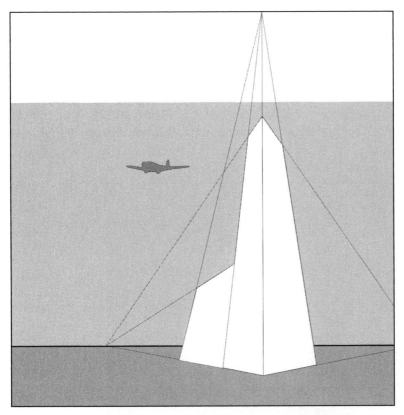

Figure 2.29 Three-point perspective helps to create extreme angles.

Often the third point is some distance from the picture, as shown in Figure 2.29. To find the third point, the artist plots the angle of the center point of the object. Notice that in the case of Figure 2.29, the line goes directly up from the middle corner of the cube. The closer the third point is to the viewer, the more extreme the angle will appear. The other lines for the sides of the cube are then drawn down from the same point.

Linear perspective is a great tool and has only been touched on lightly here in this book. The reader should take some time to study the subject in more detail.

Aerial Perspective

Air is not always clear. In fact, even on a clear day our view of distant objects is partially obscured by fine particles that float in the air. On foggy days the view may be completely blocked. Indicating this effect in art is called aerial perspective. Depending on the distance and the amount of haze in the air, objects become less distinct. Figure 2.30 shows a photograph that shows the effects of aerial perspective in nature. Notice that the flowers in the foreground are clear and sharp, and the mountains in the distance are more in the mid tones.

Figure 2.30 The photo shows aerial perspective in nature.

Reducing the contrast and detail in distant objects gives the appearance that they are more distant than objects that have higher contrast and greater detail.

Composition

There are no hard rules in composition, only guidelines. With every rule there is an example of an artist successfully breaking that rule. Rules in picture composition are a little like grammar rules in the English language. They are guidelines that can be used to help the artist create more pleasing pictures.

Balance

Basic to design is balance. If a picture is out of balance it will feel uncomfortable to the viewer. In Figure 2.31 the character is way off to the right and facing away from the center of the picture. It creates a large uncomfortable empty area in the middle and left-hand side of the picture. The picture is off balance.

Figure 2.31 The picture is off balance.

A good way to think of picture balance is to imagine that the picture is perched on a triangle. If the picture seems like it would be heavier on one side than on another, the picture will seem off balance. See Figure 2.32.

One way to solve the balance problem is to use formal balance. Formal balance is a system of balancing a picture by subdividing it into equal portions so that one side mirrors the other. Formal balance feels comfortable to us because many things in life have symmetry. Most animals are symmetrical, as is the human body. For compositions where the artist wishes to have a feeling of dignity or majesty, formal balance is a great approach. Figure 2.33 is an example of how a picture can be subdivided to achieve a formal balance.

Figure 2.32 The picture is off balance.

Figure 2.33 The lines show the formal balance of the composition.

Not everything needs to be mirrored from one side to the other, but there should be a sense of equality.

Formal balance is great for formal pictures, but because it is so balanced, the pictures can sometimes lack dynamics. Formal balance is not very good for creating pictures that give the feeling of motion or action. The artist needs to have other ways to balance a picture.

Objects or characters in a composition don't have to be equal in size or mass to balance a picture. Artists can use the principle of the fulcrum-lever in compositions. A fulcrum-lever is a like a teeter-totter. The center of the teeter-totter is the fulcrum. A heavy person can teeter-totter with a lighter person by moving closer to the fulcrum or having the lighter person move farther from the fulcrum. By placing a larger object or character near the center of the picture and placing the smaller object farther from the center, the picture will have a sense of balance. This approach to balance can add more drama to a picture. Figure 2.34 uses this method to balance the character in the foreground with the castle in the distance.

Figure 2.34 The fulcrum-lever approach can be used to balance a picture.

Focal Points

Every picture should have a focal point. A focal point is an area of a picture that attracts the primary interest of the viewer. Pictures with strong focal points are more pleasing to look at because they are not confusing to the viewer. Focal points can be achieved in several ways including lines, values, detail, and color.

One of the most effective methods of creating a focal point is to use lines in the picture. Figure 2.35 shows how the lines of the picture converge on the castle making it the focal point of the picture.

The lines in Figure 2.35 show how the design of the picture converges on the focal point. The overlaid lines just indicate the general direction of the elements. Organizing them to converge on a focal point is a design decision.

Figure 2.35 The lines in the picture converge on the castle.

It is best not to place the focal point in the exact center of a picture. Placing the focal point in the center of a picture can cause the picture to feel static. Shifting the focal point to one side or the other will help increase the dynamics of the arrangement. If the picture is a formal design, shifting the focal point to a position above center is usually the best choice.

Another excellent way to create a focal point is to use value. Value is the quality of light or dark in a picture. In Figure 2.36 the focal point is the silhouette of the knight on horseback.

To create a focal point using value, the artist places the highest contrast between light and dark at the focal point. All other images in the picture will have less contrast between light and dark.

Figure 2.36 Value can be used to create a focal point.

Detail in a picture will create a focal point. The eye is naturally drawn to areas of the picture that have the greatest detail. Figure 2.37 is a simple picture made up of mostly flat shapes. By adding a few lines of definition to the polo player, the eye is naturally drawn to the player, creating a focal point.

Figure 2.37 Detail can create a focal point.

Another very effective way to create a focal point is to use color. Okay, I know the book is in black and white, so you are going to have to imagine this one a little bit. In Figure 2.38, the background is made of colors comprising variations from blue to red. The trophy is a bright yellow and is opposite the background colors on the color wheel. It is the only color in the yellow family in the picture, causing the viewer's eye to focus on it.

Figure 2.38 Color can be used to focus the viewer's attention.

Most of the these examples are extreme to illustrate the different ways that lines, value, detail, and color can be used to focus the viewer's attention to a point on the picture. In practice, the artist should use judgment in the methods used to focus attention. The danger in being too heavy-handed with compositions is that when any technique or method of composition becomes too overbearing, the subject of the picture takes on less importance. Composition techniques should be used in such a way that they seem natural to the viewer, not contrived.

Pathways

Artists can build pathways in a picture. When scanning a picture, the human eye moves about from one area of the picture to the next. If there are natural pathways in the picture, the viewer will be able to comfortably scan the picture. If the picture lacks natural pathways, the picture will feel uncomfortable to the viewer.

Figure 2.39 shows two pictures—the one on top is the original sketch. The one on the bottom shows the paths of movement within the picture.

Figure 2.39 Pictures should have natural paths of movement for the eye to follow.

Pathways are important for keeping the viewer looking at the picture. If a pathway leads out of the picture, the viewer is apt to spend less time looking at the picture.

Summary

This chapter covered a lot of ground, from how to hold a pencil to picture composition. I hope you paid attention, because the concepts covered in this chapter are the foundation for the next few chapters in the book. Some of the important concepts we covered are as follows:

- Learning different ways to hold a pencil
- Using the whole arm to draw
- Making quick drawings
- Pencil strokes
- Shading
- Perspective
- Composition

Some of these concepts like quick drawings and shading will take some practice, while others like composition will take some study to master completely. That is, if anything in art can be mastered completely.

Questions

1. Why is holding the pencil in writing position not good for the initial steps of drawing a picture?
2. Which way of holding the pencil causes the artist to have to use his entire arm to draw?
3. Balancing the pencil is good for what type of drawing process?
4. Why is it a good idea to use a sheet of paper to rest your hand on while drawing?
5. What type of pencil stroke is good for drawing hair?
6. What type of pencil stroke uses directional lines crossing in different directions?
7. Adding areas of varying degrees of value to a drawing is called what?
8. What is a drawing created entirely of values instead of lines?
9. What type of perspective uses lines to give the appearance of depth in a picture?
10. As objects recede from view, they diminish in what quality of light and dark?
11. What causes a picture to be visually off balance?
12. Formal balance is good for what type of picture?
13. How can a large object in the foreground be balanced in a picture?
14. What is a focal point in a picture?
15. What are pathways in a composition?

Answers

1. It causes the artist to be too tight
2. The butter knife position
3. Shading
4. To keep oil from the hand away from the drawing surface
5. Weighted directional strokes
6. Crosshatching
7. Shading
8. A value drawing
9. Linear perspective
10. Contrast
11. Anything that makes one side of the picture appear heavier than the other side
12. Heroic or majestic
13. By placing a smaller object on the other side in the distance
14. A place in the picture where the eye comes to rest
15. Natural paths of movement for the viewer's eyes

Discussion Questions

1. Why is the butter knife position better than the writing position for drawing?
2. Why is it a good idea to draw lightly when first starting a drawing?
3. Why is it a good idea to protect the drawing paper from damage while drawing?
4. Why balance the composition of a picture?
5. What can happen if there are many equal focal points in one picture?

Exercises

1. Create several drawings of a game character, giving your self only 30 seconds per drawing.
2. Use two or more pencil stroke methods to draw a background for a game.
3. Design a picture using formal balance.

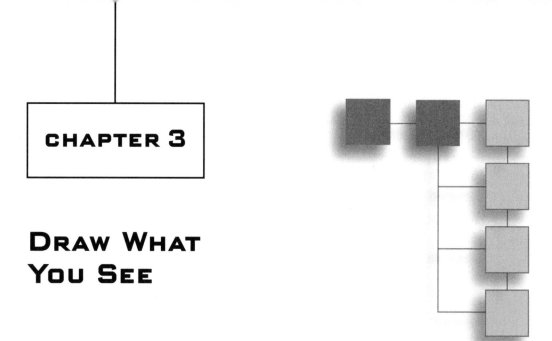

CHAPTER 3

DRAW WHAT YOU SEE

One of the most important drawing skills has nothing to do with pencil and paper. In fact, it can be done without any drawing tools or surfaces. It is learning to see.

Most people go through life without ever really seeing the world they live in. They go about their lives looking but not really seeing. That is because seeing requires more than just looking at something. It also requires understanding why things appear the way they do. For example, when a trained artist looks at a ball, he sees not only the ball but also the light and shade of the ball, including the reflected light and the shadow the ball casts. Even more than that, he will understand why the cast shadow becomes more diffused as it gets farther away from the ball and why it is slightly lighter next to the ball.

Artists learn to be observers. They learn to watch and record their surroundings in their sketch book. The artist does this not because he doesn't have a camera, but because drawing an object helps the artist understand the object's nature better.

Game artists also need to have a good understanding of the basic sciences like biology, botany, anatomy, physics, geology, math, and chemistry. Each of these sciences describes some aspect of our world. Physics, for example, explains the science of light, an important factor for the artist.

History and cultures are also important topics for the game artist. Many games are based on or derived from some aspect of human culture or history. Understanding a culture can many times inspire the game artist to create great art. Knowledge doesn't bind an artist; it expands the artist's abilities to create. The more knowledgeable the artist is, the greater his creative powers, because he has more to draw from.

This chapter will cover basic drawing and seeing skills as they relate to drawing real objects. These skills include the following:

- Scale
- Proportion
- Dimension
- Reference

The purpose of this chapter is to help you to gain skill in drawing through learning to draw what you see. Most drawing in games is imaginary characters, landscapes, or objects, but even if they are imaginary, they still need to be drawn to look real.

Scale

Scale defines how large something is. A portrait of a character has a different scale than a panoramic view of a game world. In the last chapter, we introduced linear perspective. Linear perspective is a way of organizing a drawing so that the elements look correct in relationship to one another. Even though you might be drawing a specific object using life or a photograph as reference, you still need to understand why it sits in space the way it does. Figure 3.1 shows a photograph. Next to it is an overlay with some of the perspective lines drawn in to show how the scale of the picture works. Distant elements are smaller.

Relationships Between Elements

Relationships between elements in a drawing can show how large or small something is. For example, what is the relationship between foreground and background objects in a scene? What is the relationship between a character and his surroundings?

Have you ever looked at an advertisement where there is an indication of the size of the product? If it is a small product, the picture may contain a quarter or other familiar object. The familiar object gives the viewer a point of reference to just how big the advertised item really is. Many times larger objects such as a car may include a person in the picture. If you are drawing something that is unfamiliar to the viewer, it is always a good idea to also

Figure 3.1 The perspective lines show how the scale of items is organized.

show something that is familiar so the viewer can get a sense of scale. In Figure 3.2 you see a picture of a horse. How big is the horse? It could be a big horse or it could be a pony. Unless the viewer is familiar with the markings and thus the breed of the horse, there is very little to indicate whether the horse is big or little.

Figure 3.2 How big is this horse? Copyright Peter Levius www.3d.sk

Now in Figure 3.3 not only is there a picture of a horse, there is also a person standing next to the horse. Now it is obvious that this is a large horse and not a small pony. When you set up your drawings, even if you are working from reference, you should always make sure the viewer will be able to determine the relative size of objects in your drawings.

Figure 3.3 It is easy to see that this is a big horse. Copyright Peter Levius www.3d.sk

Proportion

Proportion refers to relationships within an object or character in a drawing. In fact, proportion is all about relationships. Which is larger, a person's nose or big toe? What is the relationship between the ear and the foot of a character you are drawing? Are the monster's tentacles long or short? Each time you draw, you make decisions about proportions.

Proportion becomes extremely important when you are drawing something that the viewer will be familiar with, like a specific model of car or a human character. When drawing a person's face, for example, each feature has to conform to what the viewer expects or the face will seem awkward. This isn't to say that you can't exaggerate features to create stylized characters, but not if your intent is to be realistic. Figure 3.4 shows a drawing of a young gymnast. Because the proportions are correct, she looks like a real person.

Figure 3.4 The girl's proportions in this drawing are correct.

Now, let's do a little experiment. In Figure 3.5, I changed the facial features slightly. See if you can find the change.

Figure 3.5 The girl's features were changed.

In Figure 3.5, I moved the girl's right eye up just a little. The move was only a few millimeters, yet the result was dramatic. She just doesn't look right. Even small mistakes in the proportion of a person's head can have a big impact on a drawing.

Proportions of the Head

In Figure 3.6, the girl's head is overlaid with a few basic guidelines to help show the basic proportions of her head. The picture is of a girl around the age of nine.

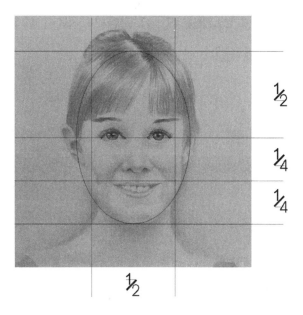

Figure 3.6 The guidelines show the general proportions of the girl's head.

The head is shown as an oval shape with dissecting lines running vertically and horizontally. The lines designate divisions of the head by half and quarters. Notice that the eyes run roughly halfway from the crown of the girl's head to the bottom of her chin. A common mistake of beginning artists is to place the eyes too high. Though every head is different, the eyes are usually about halfway. The girl may actually have more distance between the crown of her head and her eyes than between her eyes and her chin. Notice that some of her head is above the line. Much of what is above the line is hair, but not all of it. Children often have larger foreheads than adults.

Figure 3.7 shows the same divisions on an adult head. Notice the difference between the adult's head and the child's head. The adult head is smaller in the forehead, and the eyes are slightly above center.

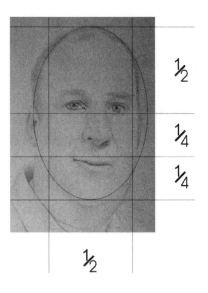

Figure 3.7 The guidelines show the general proportions of an adult head.

This may be typical of many adults versus children, but you need to be aware of the individual characteristics that make up each person that you draw. Before you begin a drawing of a person, make sure you take some time to measure the proportions of the head.

Hint

When dealing with drawing human or near-human characters, the basis for measurement is the head. Thus, artists refer to a character as being eight heads high or four heads across. The reason for measuring in heads is that it is relatively easy to measure and compare to other aspects of the body. You don't even need a ruler to measure a person. All you need is a pencil.

Hold your pencil at arms length. Sight the subject's head along the length of the pencil. Use the end of pencil to designate the top of the subject's head and mark where the person's chin ends with your thumb. You can now compare the length of the subject's head with other parts of the subject's body. Just remember to always hold the pencil at arm's length so the measurement is consistent. Bending your arm even just a little bit will throw off your measurements.

Figure 3.8 shows several heads with measurement lines. See how they are all close in proportion yet there are variations between each one?

Figure 3.8 Can you spot the variations in proportions among these people?

Proportions of the Body

In addition to the head, the proportions of the human body are also well known, and thus require the artist to understand them. Figure 3.9 shows a person from the front and back. The lines in the picture show the division of the body in heads. Notice that the character is 7½ heads high. 7½ heads is an average for most people. As a general rule, a smaller head on a large muscular character tends to make the character look more massive and heroic. A larger head on a less muscular character will tend to make the character look cuter. You can use this rule to your advantage when drawing characters, but when you are trying to draw a real person, measure to make sure you have the correct proportions.

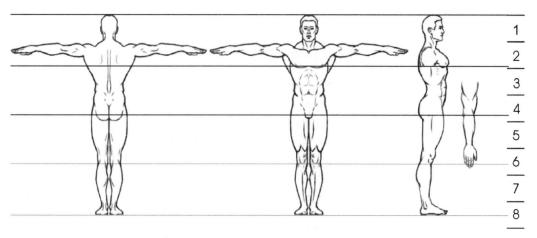

Figure 3.9 The character is 7$\frac{1}{2}$ heads high.

Notice where the figure divides in half and in quarters; these divisions will help you when you are drawing without a model. There are many divisions of the figure beyond those shown in Figure 3.9. Spend a little time getting to know the proportions of the figure.

The distance from fingertip to fingertip is very close to the total height of the figure. In Figure 3.10 the two are compared.

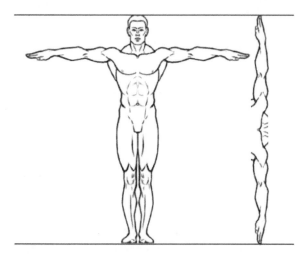

Figure 3.10 The length of the arms is equal to the height of the person.

Figure 3.11 shows the proportions for a female character.

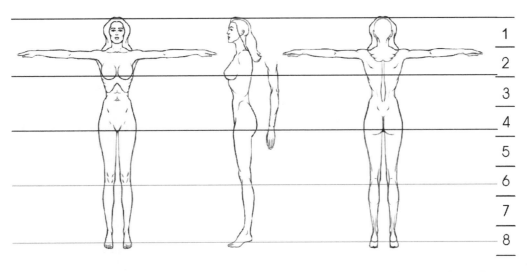

Figure 3.11 The female figure generally has narrower shoulders and wider hips than the male.

Notice that the female character is different in many ways from the male character. Her shoulders are narrower and her hips are wider. Her arms and chest are less massive, although her upper thighs are just as massive if not more massive depending on the muscularity of the character. Figure 3.12 shows a side-by-side comparison of the male and female figures.

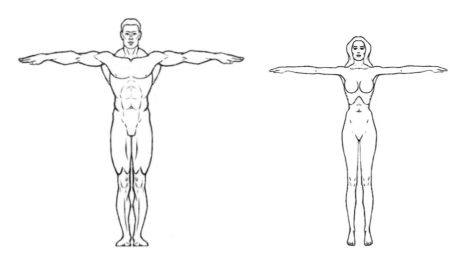

Figure 3.12 Female proportions are generally narrower than those of the male.

Actual human proportions will differ from person to person. Figure 3.13 is a front, back, and side view of a woman. Notice that she is not $7\frac{1}{2}$ heads high.

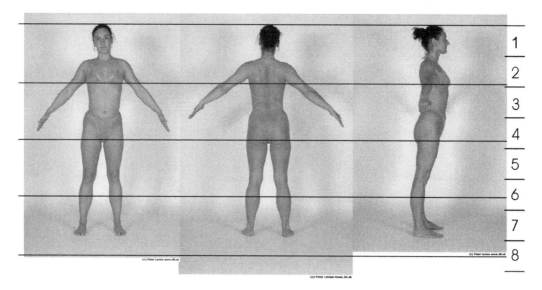

Figure 3.13 How many heads high is the model?

The model is about 7 heads high. Notice with this individual that her legs are shorter than the drawing in Figure 3.12. It is often a good idea to measure a subject before drawing to pick up on any differences in the individual's proportions.

Dimension

Dimension is related to scale and proportion, but it is a little different. Dimension as used here is drawing an object so that it appears to take up physical space. While scale and proportion can be defined entirely with lines, dimension usually needs some kind of shading to fully show it. The shading helps to define the form of elements in a drawing.

Sometimes a drawing is said to be three-dimensional, because it has the appearance of depth. In actuality, the drawing is only a two-dimensional plane. The artist creates the illusion of depth. The key factor in creating depth in a drawing is to understand light.

Light

Without a basic understanding of light, an artist will have difficulty understanding why objects appear as they do in life. The whole reason that we see anything at all is because of light. A picture without light would be easy to draw, however, because it would just be black. The minute light is brought into the scene, things begin to happen. Form and shape become distinct. Color and contrast come into being.

Properties of Light

Light has many properties. Understanding how light works on objects in a scene helps the artist to create volume to give the feeling of depth and substance to his drawings. Artists can also use light to add drama and feeling to a drawing.

On a normal sunny day our world is filled with light. Our eyes are receiving and our brain is processing light information constantly. Light can be defined as one of two types: direct light or refracted light. When we see an object, we are looking at refracted light coming from the object. When we look at a light bulb or the sun, we are seeing light from a light source (direct light).

Refraction and Reflection

Light travels in a straight path from the light source until it hits something. When light hits an object, it will do one of three things:

- Bounce off the object.
- Be absorbed by the object.
- Pass through the object.

When light bounces off an object, it is called refraction or reflection. Figure 3.14 illustrates light from a candle refracting from a billiard ball to the eye.

Whether light refracts or reflects is dependent on the smoothness of the surface it hits. Color is also a factor in reflection and refraction because color determines how much light is absorbed into the object.

Figure 3.14 Light travels from the source to an object and then to the eye.

Highlight

The highlight of an object is that part of the object that directly reflects light from the light source. Figure 3.15 shows a picture of a ball. The highlight is located in the brightest area of the ball, as shown in the picture.

Partial Light

The area that surrounds the highlight where the light is not as directly refracted is called partial light. This area extends outward from the highlight and gradually gets darker because the surface of the object is turning from the light. Figure 3.16 shows the partial light area of the ball.

Figure 3.15 The highlight is a direct reflection of the light source.

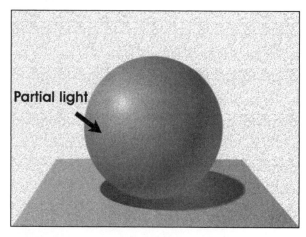

Figure 3.16 The area that receives indirect light from the light source is in partial light.

Shadow Area

As the surface of the ball turns away from the light source, it no longer receives direct light. The area that does not receive direct light from the light source is called the shadow area. Figure 3.17 shows the shadow area of the ball.

Core Shadow

There is a band of shadow that separates the partial light from the shadow area of the ball. This shadow is called the core shadow. The core shadow runs along the edge of the object that is directly past the influence of the light. It is a very important shadow for the artist because the core shadow, more than any other shading, defines the form. Figure 3.18 shows the core shadow of the ball. The core shadow is the darkest shadow on the ball, because it receives the least amount of light.

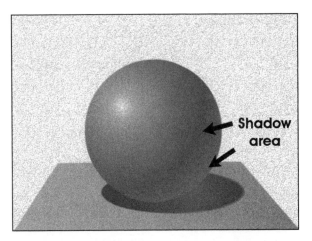

Figure 3.17 The shadow area receives no direct light from the light source.

Figure 3.18 The core shadow helps define the form of the ball.

Refracted Light

The shadow area does not receive direct light from the light source, but it does receive indirect light. Indirect light is light that is refracted from other surfaces onto the ball. Figure 3.19 shows the area of the ball that has refracted light.

Cast Shadow

Because the ball interrupts some of the light traveling from the light source to the table, there is an area of shadow on the table. This area of shadow is called the cast shadow. Figure 3.20 shows the cast shadow of the ball.

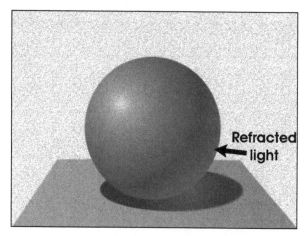

Figure 3.19 The refracted light helps to define the shadow area of the ball.

Figure 3.20 The ball casts a shadow on the table.

Cast shadows are not just flat shadows. They have unique characteristics that an artist must understand to make it look correct. As the shadow becomes more distant from the object, the edge becomes less distinct. This happens because there is more chance for refracted light to reach the shadow area. There is also a slightly lighter area just beneath the ball. This area is the twice refracted light area. Some of the refracted light from the ball goes to the shadow area, lighting it subtly.

Multiple Light Sources

Many times objects we see in life have more than one light source. This is particularly true of characters or objects in interior settings. A single room inside a building may have many lights illuminating a character or object from multiple angles. Each light will have an effect on how the character or object looks.

Exterior objects viewed during the day will tend to have only one light source because the sun is such a dominant light.

Reference

Reference is anything that an artist uses to help him visualize his work. Reference can be a photograph or a live model. It can be a location or a staged scene with props. The point is that any time an artist uses someone or something as a visual guide for a work of art, that someone or something is referred to as the artist's reference. Good artists often spend as much time getting good reference as they do working on the art itself. The more important realism is in the artist's work, the more critical good reference becomes.

Drawing from Life

Drawing from life means that the artist is looking at real objects, people, or animals as reference for his drawings. Extensive drawing from life is an important part of any video game artist's training.

There is no substitute that is quite as good as drawing from life. This is because most of us have two eyes. Because our eyes are separated from each other, each sees a slightly different view of the world. The human brain takes the two overlapping views of the world and marries them into a single view. Two views of the world allow us to discern depth, because we see slightly around objects. To see what I mean, take a pencil or pen and hold it about 12 inches from your face. Now close your left eye and visually mark the farthest you see around the right side of the pencil. Now close your right eye and open your left eye. You should notice that you can't see as far around the pencil on the right side as you did with your right eye. Even though this difference is slight, it is enough for your brain to tell how far away the pencil is from you. Computing distant objects from two points of reference is called parallax. Scientist use parallax to compute the distance of stars from the Earth.

The fact that we see the world from two points of view makes it easer for us to not only see how distant an object is but also understand more about its form. Because the artist sees slightly more than a flat single view of the subject, he can give his drawings a greater feeling of volume and depth.

Another advantage of drawing from life is that in life things move. Understanding motion from a still photograph is often difficult. In life, motion can be observed.

People Drawing

The game industry, like the film animation industry and other commercial art industries, requires the artist to be proficient at drawing people. Most art directors that I talk to look first at a prospective artist's ability to draw the human figure. The reason for the emphasis on the human figure is that it is one of the most complex and demanding subjects an artist can attempt. It is also one of the most common subjects in commercial art. Art directors use it as a measure of the artist's ability to draw because it is an easily recognizable standard for all artists. If the artist is proficient at drawing the human form, he is likely proficient at drawing anything.

Artists who wish to work in video games should spend a great deal of time learning to draw the human figure. Most college art programs include courses in figure drawing. There are also a number of good books on the subject. A quick search of the key words *figure drawing* will bring up several great resources for artists. There are literally hundreds of books on the subject, because figure drawing is as old as art itself.

A great way to learn to draw people is to take a sketch book to a public place and draw the people you observe there. Figure 3.21 is a page from a sketch book showing quick studies of people. Notice that the drawings are very simple and quick. People often don't hold still long enough for detailed drawings.

The advantages of drawing people in public places are that there is a lot of variety and no modeling fees. The disadvantage is, of course, that you can't control their movements, so detailed drawings are almost impossible.

Figure 3.21 Quick studies of people in a public place are a good practice for artists.

Another good way to draw people is to take a life drawing or figure drawing class. In these classes the artists pay to have a live model pose for drawing. The advantage to paying for models is that the artist can direct the model's movements, and the model holds a pose for long enough that the artist can work on detailed drawings.

Drawing from life is an old tradition among artists. There is a good chance that almost anywhere you live you'll find a life drawing class or a shared studio. Look up some of the art departments of your local universities or community colleges.

Drawing a Person

The process for drawing a person is different from artist to artist but there are some general rules that the beginner should follow as he starts drawing people. Figure 3.22 shows a photograph of a seated figure.

Figure 3.22 The seated model will be used as reference for the figure drawing. Copyright Peter Levius www.3d.sk.

The beginning construction lines for the drawing should be drawn very lightly so that they don't interfere with later shading. Figure 3.23 shows the initial construction lines drawn much darker than they should be. If I showed the lines as light as they actually are they wouldn't print in this book.

Notice that the lines are very loose and mostly follow the skeletal structure of the body. I draw both legs, even though one is partially obscuring the other. The lines are meant as guidelines and not as contours of the body. The initial lines should show the fundamental proportions of the figure. Once they are defined more detail can be added.

Figure 3.24 shows the drawing with more detail added to the figure. Again the lines are much darker here for printing purposes. When you do your own drawing, you should make all the lines as light as possible.

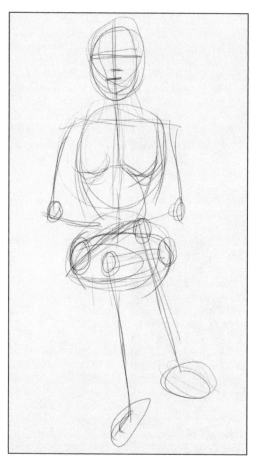

Figure 3.23 Initial construction lines define the basic position of the model's skeleton.

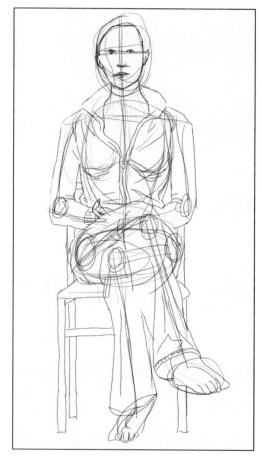

Figure 3.24 The contour and shape of the figure are defined.

Once the detail of the drawing is defined, the shading and refining can take place. Most beginning artists want to start this phase much earlier than they should. It is a much better idea to finish a light detailed figure first before you go on to a detailed shaded drawing. Figure 3.25 shows a close-up of the shading of the face. I almost always start with the head. This is a personal preference. I know some artists that prefer to start with the hands or feet or some other part of the figure. I find starting with the head helps me to develop the rest of the figure better.

There are two strong lights on the model, one on the right and one on the left. This leaves a strong shadow down the center of her head.

Figure 3.26 shows a close up of the model's foot. Notice how the shadow runs across her foot.

Figure 3.25 I like to start the shading with the head.

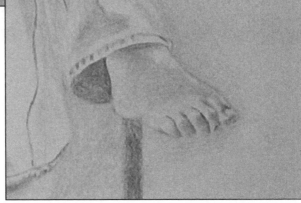

Figure 3.26 The shadows on the foot help to define it.

Figure 3.27 is the finished drawing. Almost all of the construction lines are gone. Notice how her shoulders are defined by shading behind the figure rather than a line. There could be much more detail in this drawing if it were bigger. The final drawing is only about 11 inches high by 6 inches wide.

Figure 3.27 The finished drawing is only 11 inches by 6 inches.

Using Photography

Sometimes drawing from life is impractical or impossible. Next to life, the best reference tool an artist has is his camera. A photograph is only a single view of the world, but a single view is much better than no view. Many artists keep a file, either on hard copies like prints or slides or digitally on computer files, a *morgue*. I don't know where the term morgue for reference photographs came from, but it is often used to describe these files. A large and well-organized morgue can be an invaluable tool for an artist. I started collecting photographs for my morgue when I first was studying art in college. My collection of pictures is a real timesaver.

Copyright Laws

When you draw a picture, you automatically own that picture. Your ownership is called a copyright. You can even register your picture with the government. In the US, copyright registration is handled through the Library of Congress. You can download a copyright form from the following web address: http://www.copyright.gov/forms/.

Regardless of registration, you own your own work. So does the photographer who takes a picture.

When collecting pictures for your own morgue, you should be very careful of copyright laws. The law states that every image has an owner. You should not use someone else's photograph in your work without getting permission from the owner first. If you don't get permission, you are in violation of copyright laws. Remember that the laws that give you ownership of your art are the same laws that prohibit you from using someone else's property for your art reference. It is important for artists to respect each other's work.

Several websites have collections of photographs that are royalty free, meaning that there are no usage fees that the artist has to pay to use the photographs. Some of these collections are commercial collections for professional artists and require a subscription fee. One of the best sites with the largest collection is PhotoSpin. You can look them up at the following web address: www.photospin.com.

Another great site for photo reference of objects, buildings, and surface textures is Environment Textures for 3D Artists and Game developers. Their website is at the following address: www.environment-textures.com.

Human Reference

The human body is one of the most complex and intriguing subjects for artists. Over the centuries more pictures depicting people have been created than any other subject. Learning to draw the human form well is a requirement for most video game art departments. Because of this, unless the artist specializes in environments, most game artists have an extensive number of pictures of people in their morgues.

Be aware that any picture you take of a person where the individual in the picture is recognizable will require a release from that person if they are 18 years old or older. If they are younger than 18 years of age, the release must be signed by their legal guardian. If you don't get a release for the image, you could stand to be sued. A model release form is included in Appendix A. Make sure that you retain an original of this form signed by the subject in your records if you want to use that photograph in your art.

An artist should be careful in his selection of reference for drawing people. Unless otherwise stated, the owner of a photograph holds all rights to that image and using that image as reference for a drawing is illegal. I highly recommend that you limit your use of photos to either those you take yourself or those that you specifically have permission to use. I also suggest that you only use reference that dignifies rather than exploits the human form. The last thing you want your portfolio to do is offend the art director that you want a job from.

There are numerous books, CDs, and websites that contain photographs of the human form, for anatomical information or for costume reference, specifically intended for artists to use in their studies. Use of these photographs for artistic reference is specifically granted by their owners to those who buy the books, CDs, or pay the access fees. The decision to use this material is strictly up to the individual artist. If you are interested in a serious study of the human form and feel that you need to have photographic reference to assist in your studies, please refer to the list of artist resources in Appendix A.

Summary

This chapter covered many basic principles of drawing things we observe in real life. Drawing what we see is the basis upon which beginning artists develop their drawing skills. The concepts covered in this chapter include the following:

- Scale
- Proportion
- Proportion of the head
- Proportion of the figure
- Dimension
- Light

- Refraction and reflection
- Highlights
- Partial light
- Core shadow
- Refracted light
- Cast shadow
- Reference
- Drawing people
- Using photography

Drawing what we see is a combination of seeing and understanding the world around us. This chapter is just the beginning of an exciting exploration of our world. Artists need to understand their world. They need to have a basic understanding of many of the sciences like biology, physics, anatomy, math, chemistry, and geology. They also need to have an understanding of cultures and history. As a game artist, you could be called upon to draw almost any subject. It is a good idea to have an extensive file of photo reference just in case you need to find that picture of a snapping turtle.

Questions

1. If an artist wants to understand how light works, what science should he study?
2. Drawing what we see is a combination of seeing and what other endeavor?
3. What does scale define?
4. How does linear perspective help with defining scale in a drawing?
5. How can a sense of the size of an unfamiliar subject be shown in a drawing?
6. Relationships between elements of a single object or person in a drawing refer to what drawing concept?
7. On average, a person's eyes fit where in relation to the height of the head?
8. Children generally differ from adults in the proportions of their head in what way?
9. Why do artists use the human head as a means of measuring a figure?
10. How many heads high is a normal person?
11. Why is it a good idea to measure a figure before drawing?
12. Shading helps define what about a drawing?
13. What is the highlight a direct reflection of?
14. Why is the core shadow generally darker than the rest of the shadow area?
15. Why can we see more of an object with our eyes than a camera can?

Answers

1. Physics
2. Understanding the world around us
3. How large something is
4. It helps to organize elements in a drawing
5. By putting it next to a familiar subject
6. Proportion
7. Halfway
8. Their facial features are smaller in proportion to their heads
9. It is easy to measure from any angle
10. $7\frac{1}{2}$
11. Every person is different
12. Dimension
13. The light source
14. It receives no direct light and little refracted light
15. Because we have two eyes

Discussion Questions

1. Why is the study of science important to the game artist?
2. How can learning about cultures and history help a game artist?
3. Why is it important to give a viewer a sense of the size of a subject?
4. Why is learning to draw the human figure important for a game artist?
5. What is the difference between art and pornography?

Exercises

1. Draw a scene from life using perspective to organize the elements of the drawing.
2. Draw 20 quick sketches of people in a public space.
3. Create a detailed drawing of a single individual using shading rather than lines to define the form.

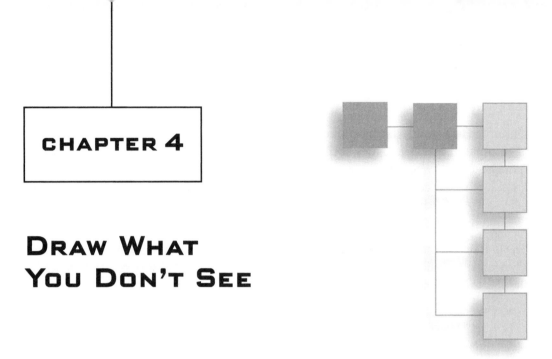

CHAPTER 4

DRAW WHAT
YOU DON'T SEE

D rawing skill is only part of what it takes to be a good game artist. In addition to being able to draw well, the game artist must also be inspired. In other words, it isn't just about how you draw, it is also about what you draw. In this chapter we will be exploring the creative aspect of drawing.

A game that has an eye-catching or unique look that draws an audience's attention is very important in the increasingly competitive video game market. If a game can stand out because it has a unique look, it could mean millions more in sales. Because of this fact, artists who have good creative skills are in high demand. This chapter will explore the following aspects of developing creativity:

- Research
- Observation
- Odd combinations
- Exaggeration
- Exploration drawings
- Distraction

Learning to turn on the creative side of your art is extremely rewarding and fun. It is challenging, but the more you work on creativity the easier it becomes. In some ways you can compare art to writing. Having good drawing skills is like knowing how to spell and use grammar correctly. But knowing spelling and grammar does not make someone a writer. It takes more than that. It takes writing something that people want to read. The same thing is true for drawing. You have to draw something that people want to look at.

Research

One of the best ways to be more creative is to be more informed. Research is a central part of creativity because it opens the mind up to new ideas. New ideas give rise to new thoughts and new visions. For example, let's say a publisher is looking for a new look for a series of sports games. The games are competing with other games that are highly realistic, so the publisher wants to make these games bolder and more exciting. A little bit of research might help solve the problem.

The first step in the artist's research will be to decide what to look for. Making a list of possible research topics is a good way to narrow the list. A possible list of research topics for the sports assignment is as follows:

- Other sports video games
- Sports highlight videos
- Sporting events
- Sports equipment
- Sports art
- Cartoons
- Comic books
- Movie trailers
- Movie posters

The list could go on much longer, but this is a good enough example for this book. Notice that the first several items on the list all relate to sports, while the later items relate more to bold and exciting. Let's look at each item to see why the artist might want to research each one.

Other Sports Video Games

Researching the competition is always a good idea. There is a good chance that the competition has already done a lot of research to come up with their designs. If you want your game to look as good as or better than your competition, you need to know what the competition looks like.

Sports Highlight Videos

Sports highlight videos are a natural research item because they show the very best in the way of sports. They also show the extremes of the sport. Highlight videos isolate the most exciting parts of a sport.

Sporting Events

There is nothing like seeing an event live to get a feel for the atmosphere and excitement of sports. Millions of people are drawn to sporting events every year. They go because it is more exciting to see the event in person. Finding a way to capture the feelings of a sporting event in a video game can go a long ways to making the game bolder and more exciting.

Sports Equipment

Researching sports equipment may not sound exciting, but there is an aspect that is worth investigating. Sports equipment manufacturers spend millions every year to capture the imagination of consumers. There is a lot to be gained by watching how they advertise and promote their products.

Sports Art

No matter what area you are researching, it is always a good idea to see what other artists have done with the subject. There is a large body of sports art. There is a good chance that some very good artists have already tried to solve the problem. It is good to see how they did it and whether or not they succeeded.

Cartoons

Cartoons are not necessarily about sports, but they are about boldness and excitement. When doing research, it is a good idea to not just look at just the subject matter but to also look at the very best art that fits the moods you want to achieve. In this case, popular cartoons fit the mood and are, therefore, a good choice to research.

Comic Books

Sports heroes are in many ways similar to the super heroes of comic book land. They may not be as powerful as the Man of Steel, but they sure seem to be stronger than the average person. Giving the players an almost superhuman feel could be very exciting for a video game.

Movie Trailers

Movie trailers are about the most exciting thing coming out of Hollywood these days. They are designed to capture our attention and tell us why we just have to see the next big movie or the world is likely to end. With that as a mission, is it any wonder that movie trailers might be a great source of inspiration for a bold and exciting sports video game?

Movie Posters

Like movie trailers, movie posters are a sales tool. Instead of showing us a movie, however, they have to entice us to see a movie with a single image. Movie posters are a great example of excitement through boldness.

Sometimes an artist just doesn't have the time to research everything that could lead to a good design for a game, but that doesn't mean that there should be no research. Research is good for all art projects that involve design. The game artist should spend a little time in research on every project.

Observation

One of the best ways to gain inspiration is to look at stuff. It is that simple. Most people never really look at things. In our lives we see thousands if not more things every day. How much do we know about the things we see? For example, feel along the edge of your jawbone. You will notice as you slide your finger along the edge that there is an indentation about halfway between the end of the chin and the back of the jaw. That small indentation is there to help protect a blood vessel as it crosses under the jaw. It also has an effect on how the jaw looks. Most beginning artists draw a rounded jaw not realizing that there is an indentation in the jawbone. Knowing this little fact will help an artist understand how to draw the jaw. It also might inspire him to design a background of a gas refinery with the same philosophy for some of the pipes or tubes.

Observation is related to research and can even be a part of research, but it is often just something that artists need to train themselves to do. Look at the world. No, I mean really look at it. See how things are put together. Watch how the clouds move. See how the water runs. Watch how animals and people move. Take time to see how the petals of a flower are attached to the stem.

Often inspiration takes time. We can't always be inspired on demand. When it does come, it is a good idea to be ready. Make it a practice to always carry a sketchbook of some kind and a pencil. That way if there is a flash of inspiration, it can be recorded.

Observation for inspiration is a little different than drawing what you see. Observation for inspiration is a creative process where the artist is trying to use the world around him to spawn creative ideas rather than examining how to draw specific objects. The inspiration may come from anything, like a shadow or the way vines hang or even the pattern created by someone's hair.

Let's say that your assignment as a game artist is to design the setting of a game that takes place in a large city. One of the goals of the game is to create a believable world that feels like a busy city with large crowds and things happening all the time.

The best way to understand what makes a city seem like a city is to go out and watch one. Look at the way people move. Look at the shops and businesses. Observe the flow of traffic through the streets. Watch the way people interact with one another. Look at the way the city is lit during the day from the sun and how it looks differently at night. Is there any one thing that makes a city feel like a city or is it a combination of many things?

Odd Combinations

A great way to increase your creativity is to put seemingly unrelated things together in a new way—for example, a knight on a chicken, as shown in Figure 4.1.

Figure 4.1 A knight on a chicken is an odd combination.

In Figure 4.1, I combined two subjects that are not commonly thought of together. The result is an interesting combination. Is the picture of a big chicken or a little knight? How do chickens fight differently than horses? If there were a game world where knights rode chickens, how would it play differently than games where knights rode horses? Combining seemingly unrelated subjects not only makes for an interesting picture to look at, it also spawns ideas for creative and interesting game situations.

Figure 4.2 shows another odd combination. This time a woman is talking to a creature behind a desk. The lizard is taking the place of what normally would be a human, thus creating an interesting game situation.

Figure 4.2 The lizard takes the place of a human in this picture.

Because the types of combinations are endless, there is an endless supply of creative opportunities. To an artist, size is not a barrier. You can take things that are normally small and enlarge them like Figure 4.3.

These are only a few examples of how odd combinations can make interesting subjects for your drawings.

So how can odd combinations be used in an actual game assignment? One place that might work is in creating creatures for a game where aliens are attacking Earth. Since there are no really good photographs of aliens, the artist needs to come up with something from her imagination. In this example, the artist might take reptiles and medieval armor and combine both with technology to come up with some unique-looking aliens. Figure 4.4 is an example of what the results of this odd combination might look like.

Figure 4.3 The dwarf is accompanied by a large rodent-like creature.

Figure 4.4 By combining odd elements, the artist comes up with a unique alien creature.

Exaggeration

Exaggeration is a good tool for increasing creativity. Exaggeration is the process of emphasizing part of the drawing by making it larger or more distinct than it normally would appear. For example, the artist might enlarge the body of a character to make it more massive or give a character larger eyes to make her look cute, as shown in Figure 4.5.

Figure 4.5 Exaggeration makes the character look cute and pleasant.

Figure 4.6 shows a sketch of a character whose arms and shoulders are exaggerated. The exaggeration gives the character a more menacing look. Also, emphasizing the eyes and minimizing the rest of the facial features adds mystery to him.

Exaggeration often works where other attempts at creativity don't. The magic of exaggeration is that it draws attention to the parts of a picture that the artist wants to emphasize. That is why it works so well. All the artist needs to do is to decide what should be emphasized and then look at how to exaggerate it.

An assignment that might work well for an exaggeration approach is to create a final boss adversary for a fantasy role-playing game. The creature needs to be the most menacing and powerful creature in the entire game. It also needs to be intelligent and resourceful.

The obvious answer for this problem is to create a dragon as the final boss, but that isn't very creative because many FRPs use dragons as their final boss creatures. Dragons, demon lords, arch manges—these are all common bosses for fantasy games. What could the artist do to create something that was more menacing yet original? Well, the answer might be in exaggerations.

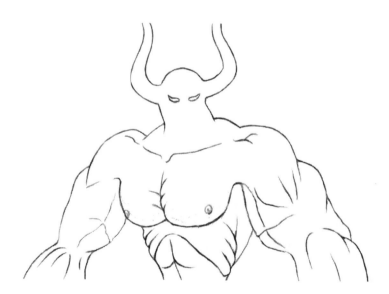

Figure 4.6 Exaggeration makes the character look mysterious and menacing.

Figure 4.7 shows a mysterious creature that is exaggerated in size, making it seem more menacing and sinister than it would if it were the same size as the hero in the foreground.

Figure 4.7 Exaggeration of size makes a normal character look like a final boss.

Exploration Drawings

Exploration drawings are what some people call doodling. The artist just starts drawing and lets the picture develop as part of the drawing process. The artist starts drawing and based on how things look, creates a picture. The idea is a little like thinking with a pencil.

Exploration drawing is pure imagination. The artist is not looking at anything other than the paper. The drawing evolves as the artist works on it. This type of drawing can be based on an idea or it can just be something created as the artist goes along.

To create an exploration drawing, you just need to take a blank sheet of paper and draw something on it. Start with a shape or a line. Then look at it for a while and imagine what kind of picture you can create from that beginning shape or line. Once you have an idea, start drawing.

Figure 4.8 is an exploration drawing of a hillbilly setting. We created these drawings with just a basic idea. The drawings evolved as they were created. In the top drawing, the boy fishing came first and the rest was created around him. In the lower drawing, the tree was drawn first but looked pretty dull so the girl and the animals were added.

Figure 4.8 Exploration drawings are creations from the artist's imagination.

Characters also can be created using the exploration technique. Figure 4.9 shows some more country folk. These characters were developed while searching for ideas for characters in the same hillbilly game design.

Figure 4.9 These characters were created using the exploration technique.

The characters in Figure 4.10 were all created from simple shapes.

Figure 4.10 These characters all started with just simple shapes.

Sometimes a picture may need to be more than just a picture of something. It needs to convey a mood. In Figure 4.11, the picture is not so much of a young girl but rather a peaceful mood.

All of the previous examples are of exploration drawings. None of them are finished drawings. They are not meant to be accurate but rather to convey an idea. Exploration drawings are almost never used as final drawings. They are idea drawings that later can be turned into finished drawings.

The best way to understand exploration drawings is to do a few. Get a sketchbook and start drawing. After awhile, you will find that this type of drawing is fun because there is no limit to your imagination.

Distraction

Sometimes it is good to just get away and think. There are times when an artist hits a wall and can't think of anything to draw. It is at these times that the artist might do well to leave the drawing board and do something else for awhile.

Figure 4.11 Sometimes the artist needs to explore moods.

A story is told of a leader with much responsibility who was one day found playing with some children by a couple of hunters. The hunters questioned the leader as to why he was playing with the children when he had so many important things to do. The leader responded by pointing to the hunter's bow.

LEADER: "Why don't you keep your bow strung all the time?"

HUNTER: "Because if it were strung all the time, the bow would lose its spring and not be as powerful."

LEADER: "The same thing is true with the mind. If I always had my mind strung tight, it would also lose its spring and become less powerful."

While simple, this story has a lot to do with creative thought. Sometimes the artist tries so hard to be creative that, like the hunter's bow, he loses his spring. He becomes less creative because his mind is too focused. The mind often needs to relax in order to be creative.

Because creativity is such an intense mental activity, the best distractions tend to be physical activities. In other words, get away from the drawing board and go out and do something like gardening, sports, hiking, yard work, or any other activity that frees the mind to think while exercising the body.

Summary

Game artists often need to draw from their imagination, because there is no good reference for many parts of a game. The game artist has to be creative. In this chapter several methods for helping the game artist develop creativity were covered.

- Research
- Observation
- Odd combinations
- Exaggeration
- Exploration drawings
- Distractions

Each of these is a method of building creativity and developing a better imagination. Not all will work for every assignment. Some will be better than others, depending on what works best for the artist. Research is the most universal and will be of benefit for the majority of projects. After researching, the game artist should then try a few of the other methods.

Questions

1. What could a unique look mean to a game in the current competitive market?
2. How does research open the artist's mind to new ideas?
3. What should the artist research first?
4. Is research important on any game project that requires design?
5. Should an artist skip research if time is limited?
6. Understanding something better can happen when the artist does what visual activity?
7. Observation uses what to help the artist be creative?
8. Combining two things that normally don't go together is called what?
9. Can odd combinations be used to create interesting game situations?

10. What is the process of emphasizing part of the drawing by making it larger or more distinct than it normally would appear?

11. Exaggeration draws attention to what part of a picture?

12. Some people refer to exploration drawing as what?

13. An exploration drawing starts with what on a piece of paper?

14. Does the artist need to have a well-planned idea to use the exploration drawing technique?

15. What type of activity makes the best diversions for increasing creativity?

Answers

1. Millions of dollars
2. It gives the mind new thoughts
3. Other similar games
4. Yes
5. No
6. Observe
7. The world around him
8. Odd combinations
9. Yes
10. Exaggeration
11. The part the artist wants to emphasize
12. Doodling
13. A shape or line
14. No
15. Physical activity

Discussion Questions

1. Why is good creative skill important to the game artist?
2. How does research help an artist to be creative?
3. Why does observation increase creativity?
4. How can odd combinations help an artist to find creative solutions?
5. What are the best ways to use exaggeration in creative drawing?

Exercises

1. Research at least five topics related to creating a dramatically new racing game.
2. Create a character for a fantasy game using odd combinations.
3. Use exaggeration to create a unique game environment.

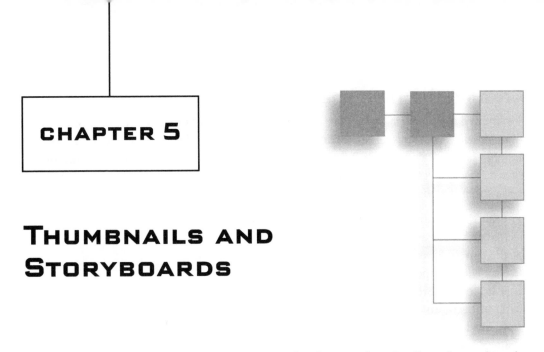

CHAPTER 5

THUMBNAILS AND STORYBOARDS

The beginning drawings in game art production are thumbnails and storyboards. Both types of drawings serve an important purpose in the development of the game. Thumbnails are idea drawing. Storyboards are production directions. In this chapter we will explore both.

Sketching Ideas

It is the job of the game artist to visualize the game. The artist must be able to see the game in his mind then communicate his vision in art. The first step in getting the vision on paper is to create small, quick sketches. These sketches are called thumbnail sketches. A thumbnail sketch is a small drawing no more than three or four inches in any one dimension.

A thumbnail sketch is not a precise drawing, but rather a quick, loose sketch of the artist's ideas. It is in these preliminary sketches that the artist begins to work out his ideas of how the game should look. In a thumbnail sketch the artist can explore multiple ideas without committing significant time to any single idea.

Thumbnail sketches are not typically part of the game design document, but rather they are used to develop the art that will be in the document. The game artist may be the only person to ever see the thumbnail sketches for a game.

Creating the Thumbnail Sketch

Thumbnail sketches are quick idea drawings used by artists to develop compositions for more detailed drawings. Often an artist will sketch several ideas in working out a larger or more detailed drawing. The following is a step-by-step approach to a quick thumbnail sketch. The subject is a subway station. In Figure 5.1 a box is drawn. It is perfectly fine to use a straightedge to build a box for your pictures.

The subway station is quickly roughed out in very light strokes of the pencil. By using very light strokes with the pencil, the artist is able to explore the drawing without becoming committed to any single line. In this way changes can be made without worrying about erasing lines. The lines in Figure 5.2 have been darkened so you can see them. In the actual drawing, the lines are much lighter.

Notice that the light outlines contain multiple lines and look somewhat sloppy. During the early stages of a thumbnail sketch the artist should not be worried about being too precise with the drawing.

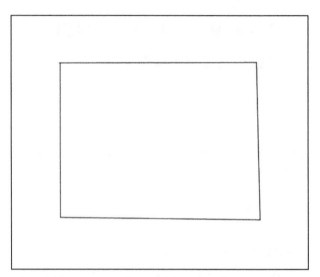

Figure 5.1 Create a box to define your drawing area.

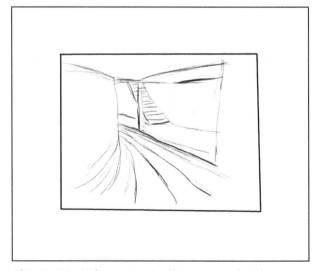

Figure 5.2 Light construction lines are used at the beginning of the drawing.

In the next stage of the drawing a straightedge is used to lay out the more mechanical areas of the station. The use of a straightedge for mechanical lines can speed up the drawing process and give the artist more control over the drawing. Curves can also be used as a guide for the artist but are more often used in more detailed rendering. The idea here is to lay out a scene as quickly as possible. Figure 5.3 shows the subway station with most of the basic lines drawn in.

Notice that some of the heavier lines do not follow the original layout. That was why the original layout was drawn in lightly.

Now the subway station is populated with passengers and a few advertisements, as seen in Figure 5.4.

This is about all that is needed in a thumbnail sketch. This drawing took only a few minutes to create and even though it is rough, the artist can get a good idea of how the scene will look from this angle.

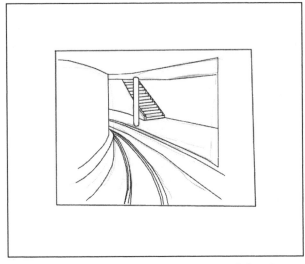

Figure 5.3 Heavier lines are used to better define the subway station.

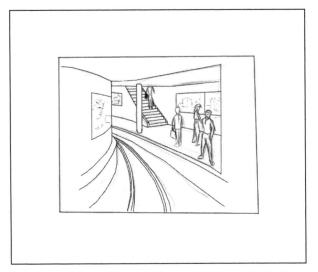

Figure 5.4 Thumbnail sketches are not detailed sketches.

In Figure 5.5 the artist is trying to work out an angle of view for a scene where a soldier is hiding from a mech. There are three different angles of view. The quick thumbnail sketches, while not very refined, still give the artist ample information for investigating different angles.

Each of the thumbnail sketches below has a different dynamic feel. The upper left sketch is somewhat static with very little tension between the foreground character and the background mech. In the middle and right-hand sketches the character's pose is more animated, adding to the drama of the scene. In both these drawings the mech is closer and drawn from an angle that makes it look more menacing. No matter how much detail is added to the first drawing, it would never have the drama and tension of the other two drawings.

Figure 5.5 The three thumbnail sketches show multiple angles of a soldier and a mech.

Thumbnails for Game Production

Thumbnails are used for many purposes in games. They can help the artist to define an idea or game element. They can be used to work out character placement, settings, values dynamics, composition, designs, and more. Because they are used to define ideas, almost anything can be drawn in a thumbnail sketch. Figure 5.6 is a page from a sketchbook showing a number of thumbnail sketches. They are all very small, measuring less than two inches in any one direction.

Figure 5.6 Thumbnail sketches are used for many purposes.

The above pictures show some of the uses for thumbnail drawings. Some are defining values. Others are designing sets. One is used to design a game title. None are very detailed.

Character Thumbnails

One of the biggest uses of thumbnail sketches is to explore ideas for characters. Characters are the focal point of a game. Having interesting characters can have a big impact on how players perceive the game. The first step in creating a good game character is to work out the ideas in thumbnail form.

The nice thing about thumbnail sketching of characters is that the artist can follow his or her imagination. The sketches are first drawn loosely as the artist searches for an idea and then refined enough to give the artist a clear picture of the major features of the character. Figure 5.7 is a thumbnail of a cartoon character. The character is much shorter and wider than a normal human.

Figure 5.7 A thumbnail sketch of a cartoon character.

One way to design a unique character is to exaggerate the character's features. In the drawing in Figure 5.7, the woman's face is very wide with a large nose and glasses that are so powerful that her eyes appear twice their normal size. If you look closely, you will see some of the construction lines.

Figure 5.8 shows a more normally proportioned character but from a sharp perspective. Looking up at the character enhances his size, making him appear to be a big character.

Figure 5.8 This character is drawn with a sharp perspective.

Sometimes it is useful to put the character in a setting to help the artist see the character in context. A setting will help to define the character and give it scale. The earlier sketches were of the character by itself. Figure 5.9 shows a character by a tree. The tree and the owl on the tree branch help to define the character as a person who lives in the forest. The spear further defines the character as a warrior.

A useful trick is to photocopy the original sketch to experiment with different options. In Figure 5.10 the fairy is copied on the paper twice. In the first copy butterfly wings are added. In the second copy bee wings are added. This saves the artist time because the fairy does not have to be redrawn and the artist can experiment with multiple wing types to find the one that works best for the game.

Figure 5.9 Sometimes a character will be drawn into a setting.

Figure 5.10 Different wings are drawn onto the copies of the fairy sketch.

Design Tool

Many artists will jump right in and finish a drawing right away. The problem with going directly to the finished drawing is that there is no plan and the drawing will suffer because not enough thought was put into the design. It is a much better idea to work out the overall design in a thumbnail sketch. Even just a few quick sketches will help the artist to define and plan a good design for a final drawing.

It is easy to change the design of the drawing at the thumbnail level because the drawings are quick and the artist hasn't made a big commitment of time or effort. If the design doesn't look good in the thumbnail sketch, chances are that it will not look good in the finished drawing either. The more design elements that an artist can work out in loose thumbnail sketches, the better the finished drawing will be.

Learning about Storyboards

A storyboard is a single panel with a picture and a description. Figure 5.11 shows a typical blank storyboard. There are two large blank areas and other smaller blank areas. Each of these areas has a purpose.

Figure 5.11 Each area on a storyboard has a purpose.

The upper large blank area of a storyboard is the picture area. This is where the game artist draws a picture that depicts the action. It usually has rounded corners to represent

the rounded corners on a TV screen. The other large blank area just below the picture area is the description area. It is here that a written description of the screen is placed. It is also here that specific directions are given.

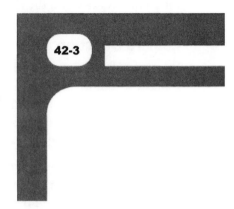

In the upper left-hand corner, there is a small box with rounded corners. See Figure 5.12 for a close-up view of the box. This box is used to indicate the number of the frame, or frame number box. Because storyboards show a sequence of actions, there are usually at least two and often several more individual panels in a series of story-boards. The series and panel number are placed in the frame number box. In the example shown in Figure 5.12, the panel is the third in the 42nd storyboard sequence.

Figure 5.12 The series and panel number are placed in the frame number box.

The long horizontal box next to the frame number box is used to indicate where the storyboard fits in the game. It is called the *scene box*. Here the artist writes the exact location of the storyboarded sequence in the game. In Figure 5.13 the sequence is in the control room of level 7.

Figure 5.13 The scene box is where the artist writes the location of the storyboard.

While simple, the layout of the story-board panel is important. The numbers in the upper left-hand corner make it easy for the team to locate any sequence. The scene box helps them to understand where the storyboard is located in the design.

This example of a storyboard panel is only one of many variations. Figure 5.14 shows another example of a storyboard panel. This panel is designed for digital development so that the entire panel can fit on a computer screen.

Figure 5.14 This storyboard panel is designed so it fits on a computer screen.

The panel has only one major area, which is divided into two sections separated by a dashed line. The scene description and directions are printed on the left of the line and the picture is drawn on the right of the line.

Camera Direction

When developing storyboard panels, you need to understand basic camera directions. Camera directions are drawn on a storyboard to tell the animator or director what the camera will be doing during a scene. For most storyboards in games, camera directions are unimportant because the player will control the camera movement. The cinematic sequences, however, require camera direction similar to storyboards for motion pictures.

The most common camera direction is the zoom, or truck, camera movement. Most people are acquainted with a zoom lens on a camera. The zoom feature of the lens allows the photographer to change how close an object or character looks in a picture. The word "truck" comes from the motion picture industry where they sometimes mount cameras on small trolleys on tracks. By moving the camera along the track, the camera can move in closer to or away from a scene. In either case, the basic camera direction is to move from a wider shot into a close-up shot. Figure 5.15 shows the storyboard direction for the zoom-in or truck-in camera action.

The edges of the picture panel represent the wide shot. The inner box represents the close-up at the end of the zoom-in camera direction. The arrows show the direction of the zoom. If the arrows are reversed, then the camera direction is reversed and the beginning shot is the close-up and the end shot is the wide shot, as shown in Figure 5.16.

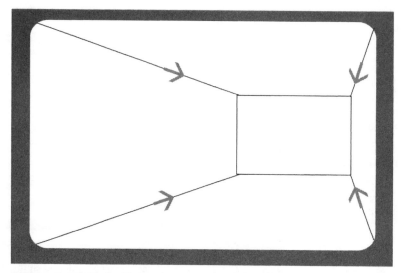

Figure 5.15 The inside box represents the end of the zoom-in in camera direction.

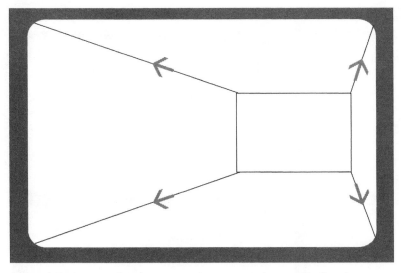

Figure 5.16 Reversing the arrows also reverses the camera direction.

Another important camera direction is pan. Pan means to move the camera parallel to the scene. Cameras can pan in any direction. Figure 5.17 shows the storyboard directions for a pan camera action.

The small box on the right is the start camera view and the two lines on the left of the box are the track of the camera as it passes over the scene. The arrow indicates the direction of the pan camera movement. The small box on the left is the end camera view.

Sometimes the camera direction will call for more than one move within a single scene. The artist can either draw several new storyboards or put more than one camera direction on a single storyboard. In Figure 5.18 the camera zooms in from an established shot and then pans from right to left across the scene.

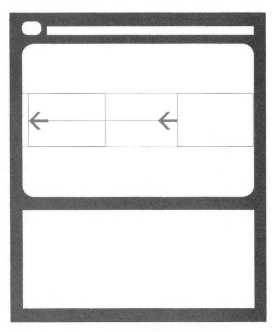

Figure 5.17 Pan is another basic camera direction.

There can be any variation on the simple camera directions of zoom and pan; it is up to the imagination of the artist. A variation that often happens is a combination of a zoom and a pan. This is shown in Figure 5.19. The camera pulls back a little as it pans across the scene.

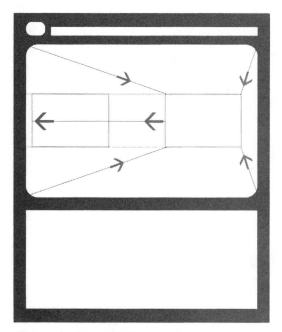

Figure 5.18 Sometimes more than one camera direction is given in a single storyboard panel.

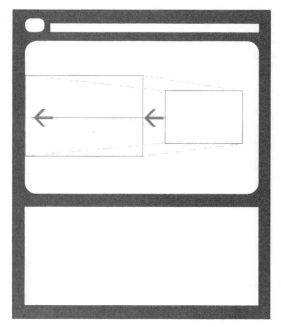

Figure 5.19 The camera pulls back as it pans across the scene.

Written Directions

In addition to drawn directions, the game artist may want to write additional direction on the panel below the picture. The additional directions help to make the storyboard as clear as possible to the viewer. For example, in the last figure the camera is moving from right to left and pulling back at the same time. The artist may want the two movements to start at different times. Offsetting movement times often will add drama to a scene. In the camera directions the artist will write the following:

> Start the pan first and then after the camera is about one quarter across the screen, start the truck out.

Typically exact frame timing is not included in the storyboards, but sometimes when the game artist is also an animator this information will be included. Usually the animation director adds the timing in the animation layout phase. If the concept artist understands timing and wishes to add some timing notes in the storyboards, the written direction would look like this:

> Hold on scene from frame 0 to frame 60, then ease in to 120-frame pan. Begin truck out at frame 90. Ease out of both pan and truck at frame 180 and hold for 60 frames.

The words *ease in* and *ease out* are terms used to indicate the gradual increase in camera speed and the gradual decrease in camera speed. Ease in will reduce the feeling of being jerked into the camera movement. The ease out direction helps to eliminate jarring stops to the camera movement.

Special Use Panels

Sometimes a scene will call for a special use panel because of the size of the scene. For example, a scene may be very wide with the camera panning over an extended portion, like in a panoramic view of the horizon. Trying to draw the scene in the standard panel would be difficult because it would be too small. Special use panels are available for just this purpose. Figure 5.20 shows a special use panel for extra wide scenes.

Figure 5.20 Wide scenes use a wide storyboard panel.

Some scenes may be more vertical in nature. For these scenes, rather than using a wide panel, long panels are available, as shown in Figure 5.21.

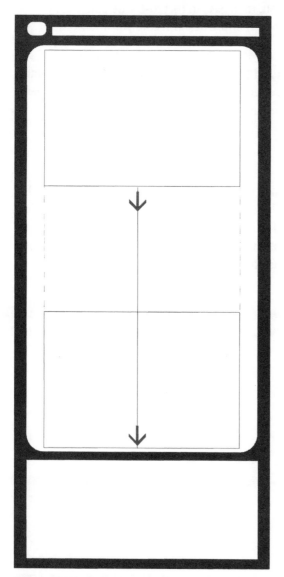

Figure 5.21 Vertical panels are also available.

In situations where the scene is very complex, the concept artist may want to have a larger drawing area. These special use panels are also available. Figure 5.22 shows an example of a larger area panel.

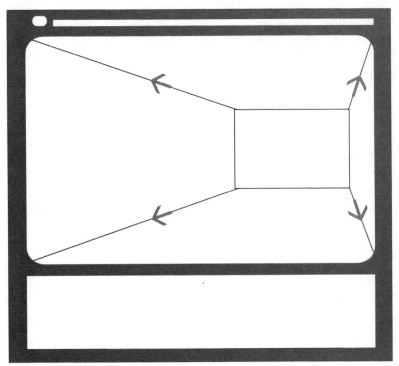

Figure 5.22 Artists can also choose a larger panel for complex scenes.

In addition to these variations, the artist can always create panels to suit the needs of the project. Feel free to copy the sample blank panels provided in this book for your own use.

Drawing Storyboards

Drawing good storyboards is a demanding task. The drawings must be simple and clear. The artist must have good drawing skills including understanding perspective, design, motion, volume, shading, and figure drawing. These skills are important in any drawing for games, but they are even more important in developing simple yet clear drawings for storyboards. Unlike thumbnail sketches, storyboards are viewed by many people on the development team. Sometimes they are also viewed by others. Often storyboards are used in marketing the game to give the fans a look into the future.

Drawing a good storyboard takes more than just good drawing skills. The artist must also understand the purpose for the storyboards. Storyboards are a communication medium, and like any other communication medium, the storyboard must tell a story. (I guess that is why they call them storyboards.) Storyboards communicate primarily through pictures. Each picture needs to show a clear image of what the game will look like. For example, a nice picture of a character in a corridor from an extreme angle may look great, but will the character ever be seen from that angle in the game? If not, then the picture is not filling its role in the design.

The following section will show you how to draw good storyboards.

Creating the Storyboard

Even though a storyboard is more complex than a thumbnail, it still starts as a thumbnail. Figure 5.21 shows one of the thumbnails from Figure 5.6.

Figure 5.21 The first step is to create a thumbnail sketch.

The thumbnail shows an idea of a game character hanging from a ledge. Another character is looking down from the ledge. In the storyboard this idea will become more defined. Using the thumbnail as a guide, draw in some of the initial defining lines. These lines are usually drawn in very lightly. They are drawn in darker here so they show up in print. Figure 5.22 shows these beginning lines.

Notice that these beginning lines define movement and shape but do not indicate proportions, depth, or detail. These lines are mainly to get something down on paper as a guide for more detailed lines later. Figure 5.23 is a continuation of the beginning defining construction lines.

Figure 5.22 The initial lines are sketched in lightly.

Figure 5.9 Sometimes a character will be drawn into a setting.

As the drawing progresses, more definition is added to the characters and their surroundings. The characters are primarily skeletons and the surroundings are just vague definitions. In Figure 5.24 the foreground and background are added.

Once everything is defined lightly, specific detail can then be drawn over the more complex areas to define them more clearly. In Figure 5.25 the contours of the hanging character are better developed.

Figure 5.24 All the major elements are lightly defined.

Figure 5.25 The character's body is better defined.

Once the picture has progressed to the point that all of the construction elements are in place and the more complex areas are loosely defined, specific detail can be added. Figure 5.26 shows some of the detail added to the main character. Notice that the construction lines are much lighter, as they should be in the real drawing.

Continue to work on adding detail to all elements of the drawing. The focal point should have more detail than in other areas. Figure 5.27 shows the drawing as it nears time for adding value.

Figure 5.26 Detail is worked in only after the construction lines are complete.

Figure 5.27 More detail is added to the picture.

In some drawings value is added with the detail. In others it is added as the last step. A lot depends on the way the artist likes to work and the media used. If the artist is using watercolor or ink washes, they are usually added at the end after all of the pencil work is finished. If the artist uses only a pencil, then value can be added as the drawing progresses. In this example, the value is drawn in as the last step, as shown in Figure 5.28.

Figure 5.28 Value is added as the last step.

The Storyboard as a Series

A storyboard drawing is usually only one of many pictures in a series. A game is often broken into specific levels, and each level is then broken down into sections. The storyboards break each section into sequences. A sequence may or may not have multiple storyboard sets. Because storyboards are used to describe an event, they usually will have two or more panels in a set. In the following example the storyboard set is broken into four separate panels.

In this set, the four panels will describe the heroine entering a room, discovering an enemy hidden in the room, defeating the enemy, and investigating the area where the enemy was hidden. Figure 5.29 shows the early thumbnail sketches for the series of panels.

Figure 5.29 The first step is to create thumbnails for each panel.

In the thumbnails, the artist works out the basic design of each panel. The game is a third-person game, meaning that the main character is viewed onscreen as opposed to seeing the game through the character's eyes. This limits the design in many ways, but it is still possible to come up with some interesting compositions.

Once the artist is satisfied with the composition of each thumbnail sketch, work on the actual panel can commence. Figure 5.30 shows one of the storyboard panels roughed in very lightly.

Figure 5.30 The initial panel is roughed in lightly.

It is important to not be too tight with the drawing in the initial stages. A looser, more fluid approach tends to help give the drawing a better feel. By not committing to any given line, the artist is able to feel the shapes as they are created. The loose initial drawing may change dramatically before the panel is finished, but drawing lightly helps get the artist past the blank sheet of paper that often stymies creativity.

Once the drawing is roughed in, the artist can then start work refining the shapes. In Figure 5.31 a straightedge was used to draw in the lines for the large blocks of the hall.

Notice that the lines are still relatively light. At this stage the artist should still be searching for the right proportions of the figure and other objects in the environment. In this example, the perspective lines converge on the center of the heroine's back. This design element helps to center the viewer's attention on the main character in the panel.

As the drawing becomes more refined, the lighter construction lines give way to the slightly more defined lines of the actual objects and characters. The construction lines are still there, but they are less noticeable as the heavier lines are drawn in. If some of the construction lines are too noticeable, they can be erased using a kneaded eraser.

In Figure 5.32 the drawing is well defined. Notice that the pool in the room is lowered in this drawing. That is because it does not match the perspective of the walls.

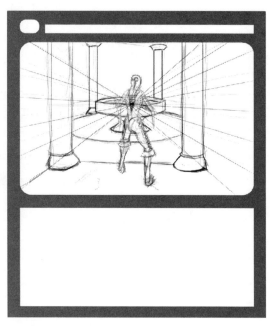

Figure 5.31 The shapes in the drawing are refined.

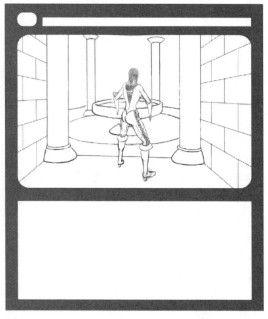

Figure 5.32 The pool is lowered to match the perspective of the hall.

Hint

If the artist is using a digital drawing program, erasing and cleaning a drawing is not a problem. If the artist is using a pencil and paper, then she needs to be very careful because erasing can cause damage to the surface, resulting in problems when the artist starts shading.

After all the major lines of the drawing are in place, the artist can then start the shading process. It is usually a good idea at this point to do a quick thumbnail sketch like the one in Figure 5.33 to define the values that will be used in the drawing.

The final stage of the drawing is to add the shading. Shading a storyboard can be done with a pencil or with other media like markers, watercolor washes, or drawing pastels. The artist should experiment with different media to see what works best. Figure 5.34 shows the sketch with shading.

Figure 5.33 Draw a quick thumbnail value sketch to help define the values.

Figure 5.34 The last step is to add shading to the drawing.

The storyboard drawing is now complete, but the storyboard is not finished yet. The written information still needs to be added before the storyboard is finished. Figure 5.35 shows the completed storyboard with the written information.

Figure 5.35 Finish the storyboard by adding the important written information.

Now that the first panel is finished, the artist can go on to the next panel in the series. Try drawing some of the remaining panels yourself. You can use the thumbnails in Figure 5.29 as a starting point, or you can create your own.

Digital Storyboards

Today a good percentage of storyboards are developed digitally using a drawing program. In the following example, the storyboard is created entirely on a computer. Drawing on a computer is much like drawing on paper, if you have the right hardware. I like to use a Wacom Intuos tablet. Figure 5.36 shows the Intuos tablet in use.

The tablet uses a stylus pen that weighs and feels a lot like a pencil. It is pressure-sensitive so it reacts similarly to a real pencil. The tablet is nice because it can be held in any position like a sketchbook.

Figure 5.36 Use a tablet for digital drawing. (Photo courtesy of Wacom Technology. All rights reserved.)

New touchscreen technology is also available for those who want to work directly on the screen. Figure 5.37 shows the Wacom Cintiq tablet/monitor in use.

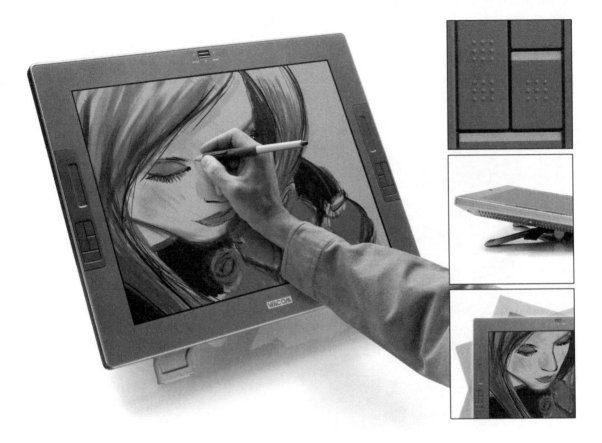

Figure 5.37 New technology allows artists to draw directly on screen.
(Photo courtesy of Wacom Technology. All rights reserved.)

The storyboard in this demonstration will consist of three panels of a ninja character shooting an arrow at a target. Figure 5.38 shows the panels roughed in using Corel Painter.

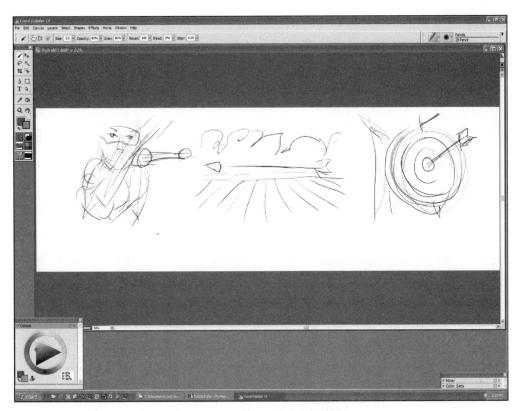

Figure 5.38 The storyboard panels are drawn using Corel Painter.

After the panels are roughed in, the storyboard frames are added to define the drawing space for each panel, as shown in Figure 5.39.

Figure 5.39 Drawing spaces are defined.

Now that the drawing area is defined, the artist can draw in the detail of each panel over the roughs, as shown in Figure 5.40.

Figure 5.40 A more refined picture is drawn over the roughs.

One of the nice parts of working in digital media is that you can erase all you want without hurting the surface. This means that the artist can draw without worrying about the lines being wrong because changes will not harm the drawing surface. Figure 5.41 shows the drawing after the construction lines are removed.

Figure 5.41 The construction lines are erased.

Focusing on the first panel, a pattern is drawn into the bow, as shown in Figure 5.42.

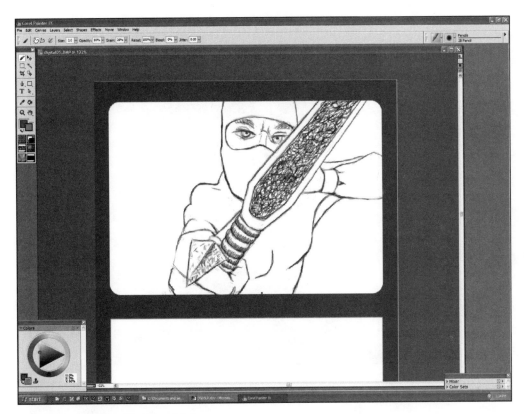

Figure 5.42 More detail is added.

Enlarging the pencil brush helps to shade a drawing quickly. Figure 5.43 shows the first panel after shading is applied.

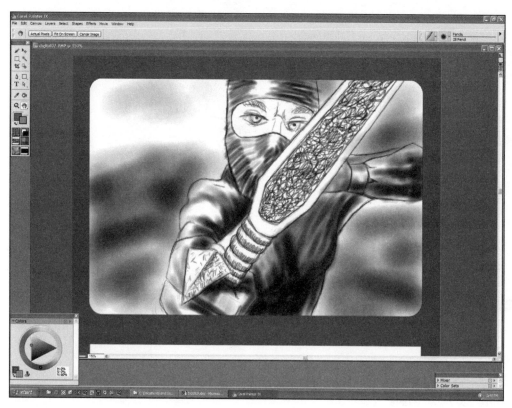

Figure 5.43 The picture is shaded using a large pencil brush.

Shading is also added to the other two panels. In addition, simple explanations are printed in the white description areas of the storyboards. (See Figure 5.44.)

Figure 5.44 Finish the other two panels.

As you can see, there is not a lot of difference in the technique for drawing storyboards on paper versus digitally. The advantages of digital drawings are many but the biggest might be that they don't have to be scanned into the computer.

Summary

This chapter covered the creation of thumbnail sketches and storyboards. Topics included the following items.

- Creating thumbnail sketches
- Creating thumbnail sketches for games
- Creating thumbnail sketches of characters
- Understanding storyboard panels
- Creating camera directions on storyboard panels
- Drawing storyboards
- Drawing storyboards digitally

Thumbnails sketches are the beginning point of drawing for games. They are used to quickly show ideas. Storyboards are used to show sequences of action in a game. They are often seen by many people, whereas thumbnail sketches are typically only seen by the game artist.

Questions

1. When are light pencil lines used in creating a thumbnail sketch?
2. Usually the first sketch is the best, so an artist rarely needs to do more than one or two thumbnail sketches. (True or False)
3. Are thumbnail sketches used much in character designs?
4. How can copying a thumbnail sketch help an artist to experiment with character designs?
5. Should an artist use thumbnail sketches to plan the design of a picture?
6. What is the frame number box used for in a storyboard panel?
7. What is the scene box used for?
8. How does the artist indicate a camera movement from a wide shot to a close-up shot?
9. What direction is used for moving the camera from one side of a scene to another parallel to the scene?
10. A long horizontal storyboard panel is used for what purpose?
11. What should an artist sketch before shading a picture?
12. Are storyboards usually single drawings or part of a series of drawings?
13. When should the artist start working on detail in a storyboard?
14. How are computers used to create storyboards?
15. Why is erasing less of a problem on a digital drawing than a paper drawing?

Answers

1. At the very beginning of the drawing
2. False
3. Yes
4. The artist can experiment with detail without having to redraw the drawing.
5. Yes
6. To indicate the panel number and the set number
7. To show the location of the set of panels within a game
8. By using the zoom-in or truck-in camera direction
9. The pan camera direction
10. To storyboard wide scenes
11. A value sketch
12. Part of a series of drawings
13. After all of the picture elements are sketched in lightly
14. To make digital drawings
15. Erasing will not cause problems with the surface of a digital drawing

Discussion Questions

1. Why shouldn't an artist spend a lot of time working on a thumbnail sketch?
2. Should an artist put a lot of detail in a thumbnail drawing?
3. Why is it important to use storyboards in developing animation?
4. How can storyboards be used to show emotion?
5. Why are storyboards better than thumbnail sketches for showing a sequence of events?

Exercises

1. Create several thumbnail sketches of a wizard for a game. Try different clothing and genders as well as different creatures to find the best design.
2. Create an opening cinematic for a game using a series of storyboards. Use at least two major camera movements.
3. Create a series of storyboard panels that describe a character's encounter with a major game enemy.

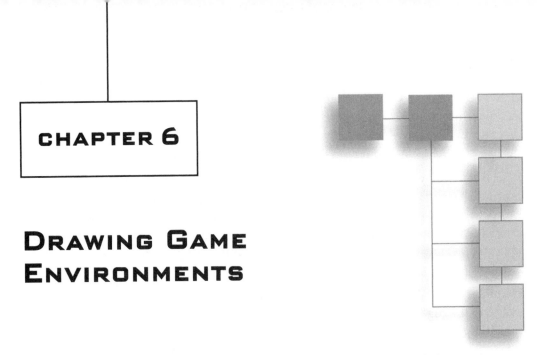

CHAPTER 6

DRAWING GAME ENVIRONMENTS

Two types of drawings are usually required for environmental designs in game development: level layouts and level illustrations. This chapter will cover both types of drawings and explain how they are developed. It will also cover the purposes for these drawings in the game development process.

Level Layouts

Level layouts are the road maps to the levels in a game. They are used to define and organize the elements in levels. This section will explore level design and show how level layouts are used in the creation of a game. It will include the following information:

- Description of level layouts
- How level layouts are used in game development
- What information they contain
- How they are created

Later in the chapter I will cover level sketches, which are pictures of areas in a game level.

What Are Level Layouts?

A level layout is a scale drawing of a level used as a guide by the development team to create a level in a game. Level layouts are drawn to scale because they need to be accurate. The development team will be using them as a guide for creating the level artwork.

Unlike other game art, level layouts are not concerned with artistic composition. They are working drawings so the main focus is for clarity and communication. This isn't to say that the drawing doesn't have to look good. It just means that the artist needs to focus on the needs of the game and not on the composition of the picture.

Level layouts are where the specific play elements of the game are designed. When creating a level layout, the paramount consideration is given to developing a fun game. All elements in the layout should be placed to create a fun experience for the player. For example, if a game is a side-view platform game, the distance a character can jump is important. Figure 6.1 shows a section of a level layout for a platform game.

The character's jumping distances are shown with a dotted line. The large vertical shaft in the center of the drawing is too wide for the character to jump unaided. A springboard placed at the edge of the shaft can propel the character over the shaft if he makes a running jump from the crate. Notice the stalactites along the roof of the cave. If the player times the jumps wrong, he is likely to hit one of those. Once over the shaft, the player will need to stop the character's forward momentum or risk being smashed by the pistons. In this section, the character has to time his movement to avoid being crushed. The level layout explains all of these things visually.

From this example it should be evident that the level layout defines the level in great detail. Level layouts are usually collaborations between the game designer and the game artist. The designer will sometimes create rough sketches on graph paper, which the artist must interpret into the layouts.

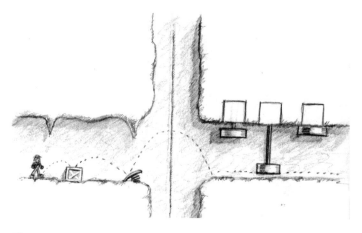

Figure 6.1 Jumping distances are shown with a dotted line.

Using Level Layouts in Game Design

Because level layouts contain extensive detail, they are used for many purposes in the course of game creation. The most common, of course, is to convey the level designs to the development team. Another equally important use of level layouts is to determine the assets for the game. In addition, layouts are also used to define story elements, place characters and objects, locate events, and define paths.

Level Designs

When creating a level, the development team builds all the elements that go into it. The development team will use the level layouts as templates to create the levels. Figure 6.2 shows a level layout for a racing game.

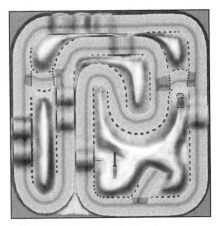

The layout is drawn to show the hills and jumps on the track. In Figure 6.3 the layout is being used as a template to guide the development artist in creating the track. Notice the wire-frame model above the track. It shows how the model was created from the original layout. Using level layouts as a template for the creation of the level is a common practice in game development. If a level is not drawn to scale, the modelers have to interpret the level. It is much better to work out the details on paper first. Modeling is expensive and time consuming.

Figure 6.2 Layouts for levels need to be accurate.

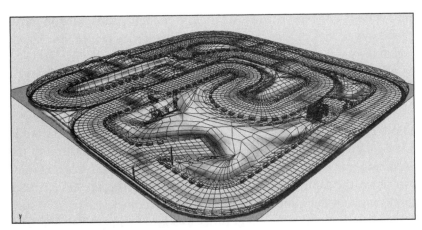

Figure 6.3 The layout is used as a template.

The model may not always follow the layout exactly because there will always need to be game adjustments. Even the best layout artist can't anticipate every part of a game. However, the layout is the base for the model, and without it the development team will have no concrete guidelines for developing the game worlds.

Asset Count

Developing a game is an expensive endeavor. One of the major costs is the creation of all the game assets. Game assets are the graphics and audio elements used in creating the game. This includes the game worlds, characters, objects, vehicles, creatures, weapons, effects, and all audio files. Basically any art or audio used in the creation of the game are considered game assets even if they are not actually used in the final version. Costs for creating game assets can run in the millions of dollars for some games. It is, therefore, important to be able to predict the amount of assets a game will require in advance of beginning development.

The level layout is a big tool for the game designer to use to determine an asset list to include in the final design. The painstaking detail of a level layout is ideal for determining the number and complexity of graphic and audio files necessary for each level. All the designer needs to do is go over the layout and write down all the game elements. For this reason, a level layout needs to include everything in a level.

Level layouts will generally contain a legend that describes elements in the layout. Figure 6.4 shows a safari game. A legend on the side of the layout gives more specific information about the symbols used in the layout. A legend is a written list that corresponds to symbols or other art used in a layout.

As you can see from Figure 6.4, the layout looks a lot like a road map. Thinking in terms of a road map is a good way to look at level layouts because like a road map, a level layout is a map of each level of the game. It shows how the player navigates through the level and all of the things the player finds along the way.

Define Story

Many games have story elements. The level layout is where the designer orchestrates the progression of the story. In a level layout, the designer can plan for the regulation of the game, plant story elements, and create a series of events that will propel the story forward in the game. If for instance, the game is about finding a buried treasure, the designer can give the player clues throughout the game. The clues are placed in the level layout in such a way that the player has to discover each one in order to solve the mystery of the treasure's location.

Safari Rally level 4

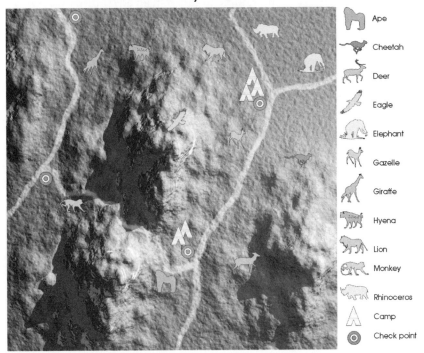

Legend:
- Ape
- Cheetah
- Deer
- Eagle
- Elephant
- Gazelle
- Giraffe
- Hyena
- Lion
- Monkey
- Rhinoceros
- Camp
- Check point

Figure 6.4 The legend gives more specific information about layout elements.

The designer can limit access to some areas of the game based on the completion of a specific event. In the game layout, the designer can place an event that will trigger another event and refer to both in the legend to show that one thing has to happen before another.

Placing Characters and Objects

The game layout will indicate locations of characters and objects. As part of the game layout, the designer will show where a character or object will be located. It is important to place the characters and objects in the level layout because they are the interactive features of the game.

If the game is a military game, for example, the placement of enemy forces is critical to the play of the game. Too many enemy soldiers in a location and the player will not be able to defeat them. Too few soldiers and the player will not have any challenge. With a level layout, the designer can see if the characters are placed too close together.

Objects like characters are also important, particularly where the object is important to the overall progression of the game. A good example of this is in an adventure game where the player has to gain a key to unlock the door to the next level. It is important that the key is neither too easy nor too hard to find.

Placing Events

Events are also placed in a game layout. An event is something that will happen that affects the game. For example, a mystery game may have a clue to a murder but it is only available after the player talks to a specific character and asks a specific question. The asking of the question is a game event that triggers another game event. These events can be added as symbols in the layout and then described in the layout legend or other supporting documentation.

Other events may be environmental changes. A golf game may have a random occurrence of rain on any given hole. The event is a random weather system and it should be included in the level layout with information on how it works.

There are any number of events that happen in a game. Defining them in the level layout is the best way to keep track of them. In the layout the designer is able to see to it that no one area is too overcrowded with events while others have too few. The game artist needs to work closely with the game designer to define the placement of any game event.

Defining Paths

The designer can use level layouts to define the path of a player through the game. Game paths are the possible ways a player can move through a game. Some games, like fantasy role-playing games, are very open and allow the player to wander about with no real path of progression. Other games, like circuit racing or puzzle games, may have a predetermined path of progression that the player must navigate to complete the game.

Game paths are defined in the level layout. For example, in an adventure game the player may need to have a certain level of armor to protect it from the attack of the dragon. The designer can set up the game so that the player has to go through a canyon to reach the dragon's cave. Along the way to the cave the player discovers the bones of an ancient warrior. The needed armor is there for the taking. Thus the designer has created a path to the dragon that crosses a necessary event. The canyon is the path.

There are lots of ways to create paths in a game. Paths can be set in stone so the player has very little choice or they can be very open and flexible with the guidance as suggestions rather than commands. In the case of the dragon and the canyon, the player has no choice. The only way out of the canyon is to kill the dragon. In another game, the dragon's cave may be approachable from any number of directions, leaving it up to the player how he will approach the cave.

Single-path games are easier to design than multipath or open-path games, because with the addition of each new route possibility, the designer and artist have to establish how the player will be able to still achieve the game objective. Sometimes the paths seem open, but they are really not. In this instance, the layout is more like a maze. All the paths except for one lead to dead ends.

Information in Level Layouts

Level layouts contain extensive information about the specifics of a given level. To create a good level, the designer has to visualize the game and play it in his mind. Each important facet of the game needs to be recorded. The level layout is where the game artist records the information.

Level layouts are ideal for storing information because they are both a visual and a written document. The visual aspects of the document allow the designer to place things in a game by location. The items placed can be actual objects or characters seen in the game, or they can be elements like events that are not seen in the game but still have an affect on the game. The written portion of the document describes the items placed in the layout and allows for the designer to add the element of time or progression.

A level layout is a detailed document. The more information it contains, the better the development process, because there will be less left to chance. In the layout, the designer creates a paper version of the game and works out many of the problems. The layout gives the designer a chance to see the game in a map-like format so that the gameplay can be balanced.

In Chapter 4, the concept of compositional balance was introduced. Like compositions, games need to be balanced as well. A balanced game will be more fun to play because the game elements are orchestrated to give the player the best possible game experience. The game will progress in a natural way. The challenges in the game will be within the scope of the player's skill. The game will not have glaring flaws that allow the player to circumvent important game aspects. In the level layout, the designer can work on balancing the game on paper before it is put into production.

Creating a Level Sketch

Before an accurate level layout is drawn, the artist will usually draw a sketch of the level. The sketch can be rough or it can be detailed. In the following example, the layout sketch is drawn to scale to help define the game area of a mountain racecourse. The course has many roads that connect with each other. The layout sketch will be used by the design team to define the possible racecourses for the area.

1. The sketch is drawn on a sheet of grid paper, as shown in Figure 6.5.

2. The first step will be to draw in the roads, as shown in Figure 6.6.

3. After the roads are drawn, the water is drawn indicating where it crosses the roads. A lake is also drawn in. See Figure 6.7.

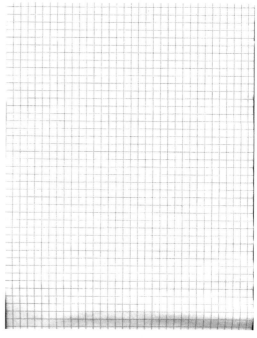

Figure 6.5 Start the sketch on a sheet of grid paper.

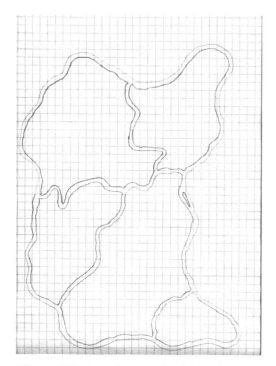

Figure 6.6 Draw the roads for the level.

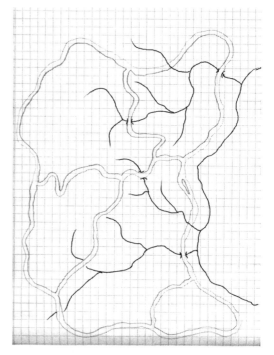

Figure 6.7 Draw the water for the level.

4. Using the rivers as a guide, shading is added to indicate elevations, as shown in Figure 6.8.

5. Part of the course will be through a wooded area. The trees are drawn to show the wooded area. See Figure 6.9.

6. The final elements are a small wooded area near the bottom of the level sketch and a marsh area near the top. See Figure 6.10.

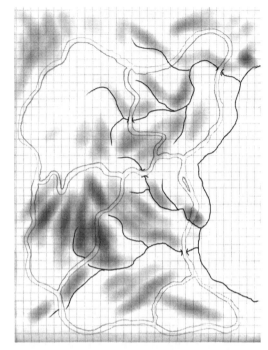

Figure 6.8 Use shading to draw the mountains.

Figure 6.9 Draw the wooded area in the center of the level sketch.

Figure 6.10 The sketch is completed.

Creating a Level Layout

The first step in creating a level layout is to define the area that the level will include. For this example, let's assume the game level will be the top floor of a hunting lodge. The lodge will have many guests that the player will need to meet and talk to during the course of the game. The top floor of the lodge needs to contain a secret room, a library, a lounge, a piano room, a bathroom, a kitchen, and some guest rooms.

Level layouts can be drawn by hand, but most of the time they are drawn digitally. Programs like Adobe Illustrator or Corel Draw are great for creating level layouts digitally on a computer. Drawing on a computer is sometimes easier when you need to draw to scale.

Start by drawing a rectangle that will define the outer dimensions of the level, as shown in Figure 6.11.

The level layout for this level will look very similar to a simple floor plan. Not all level layouts will look like floor plans, but thinking of them as such can be very useful because, like floor plans for a home, the developers of the game will use them to construct the level.

The rooms are drawn in, as shown in Figure 6.12. Smaller guest rooms are drawn in the top of the drawing while larger common rooms are drawn in the lower part of the drawing. Openings for doors are included.

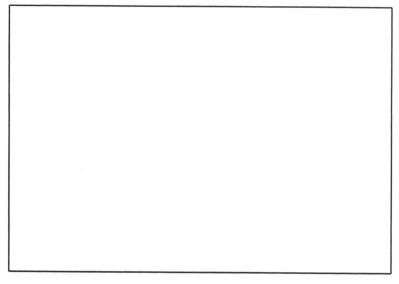

Figure 6.11 Define the size of the level by drawing a rectangle.

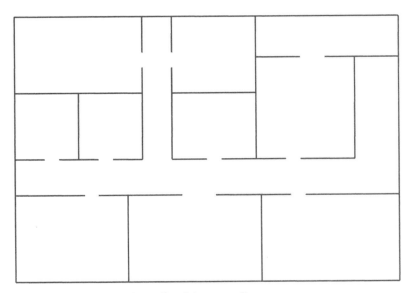

Figure 6.12 Draw in the walls of the upper floor.

This is the upper floor of a hunting lodge. The players need a way to get their characters from the bottom floor to the top floor. A staircase is added to the drawing on the right-hand side, as shown in Figure 6.13.

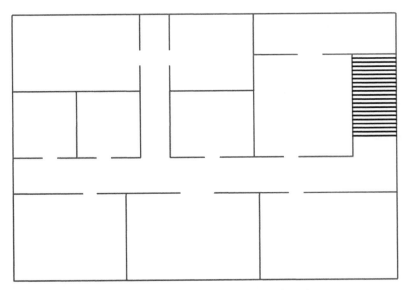

Figure 6.13 Add a staircase to the right-hand side of the layout.

All good hunting lodges need doors. Doors are added to each room. When creating objects that are duplicates of each other like doors, each one does not need to be created individually. Drawing programs like Adobe Illustrator or Corel Draw allow the artist to create an object and replicate it as many times as needed. If the drawing is created by hand, the artist can build an object and then photocopy the object and make several copies that can be pasted to the drawing. Another option is to cut a template from a heavy piece of card stock and use it as a drawing guide. Figure 6.14 is the door object. It is created with two heavy lines to show the door's open and closed positions. A lighter line arches from the heavier lines to show the swing of the door.

Figure 6.14 The door symbol is made up of three lines.

Figure 6.15 shows the doors for all the rooms, including the secret door to the secret room. Notice that all the doors are symbols, but they are still drawn to scale.

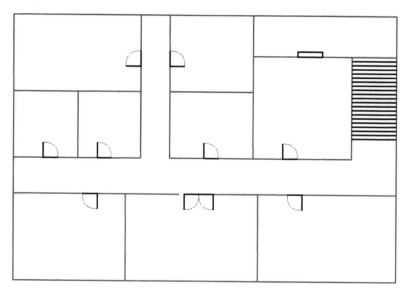

Figure 6.15 Add the doors to the drawing.

The next step is to put the furniture into the room. Many drawing programs will have symbols in their font libraries for floor plans. In addition, symbols can be bought from your local architectural supply store. Figure 6.16 shows the piano room with some couches, a chair, and a few other furnishings. The symbols for each are all part of the symbol library in a drawing program. If the artist wishes to create her own furniture items, she can do so in the same way that the door was created. Even with the use of symbols, the items need to be scaled to accurately fit the layout.

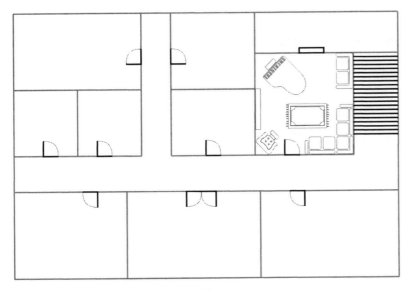

Figure 6.16 Add furniture to one of the rooms.

The rooms on the upper portion of the drawing are mostly guest rooms and several have beds. The secret room is located just above the piano room where it will be more difficult for the player to detect it in relation to the other rooms, because it is located next to an exterior wall. Figure 6.17 shows these rooms added to the layout.

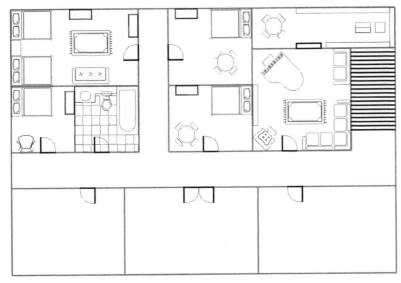

Figure 6.17 Add furniture to the rooms in the upper portion of the layout.

Continue to add furniture, as shown in Figure 6.18, to the rest of the lodge.

The lodge needs a floor to keep the characters from falling into the level below. Add a floor under the furniture by drawing light lines to indicate hardwood flooring. With a floor in place, it is possible to also add some shadows to give the layout more depth, as shown in Figure 6.19.

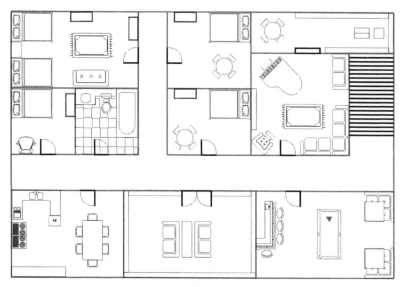

Figure 6.18 Furnish each room in the level.

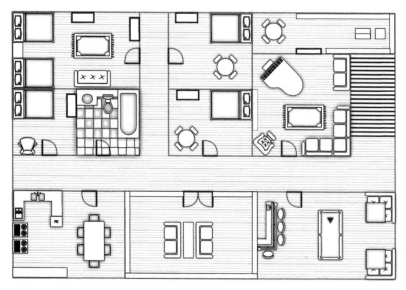

Figure 6.19 Add a floor and some shading.

This game is an adventure game. The player must interview other people in the level to get information. The next step in the level layout will be to add the characters. Again a symbol is created to represent each character. Figure 6.20 shows the characters added to the layout.

The characters are numbered and a list of the characters is added to the layout. Refer to Figure 6.21. The list is the layout legend.

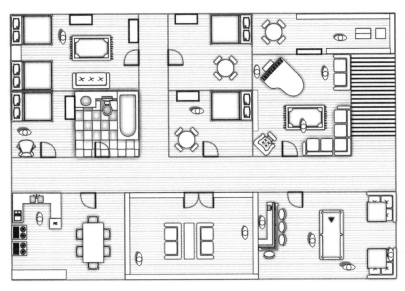

Figure 6.20 The characters are added to the layout.

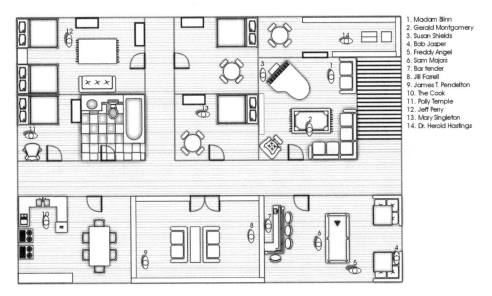

1. Madam Blinn
2. Gerald Montgomery
3. Susan Shields
4. Bob Jasper
5. Freddy Angel
6. Sam Majors
7. Bar tender
8. Jill Farrell
9. James T. Pendelton
10. The Cook
11. Polly Temple
12. Jeff Perry
13. Mary Singleton
14. Dr. Herold Hastings

Figure 6.21 Numbers are added to identify the characters.

Some games will have characters and objects that need to be listed in the layout legend. The legend is the numbered list by the picture. It can contain any important game information. Figure 6.22 shows the addition of the objects.

1. Madam Blinn
2. Gerald Montgomery
3. Susan Shields
4. Bob Jasper
5. Freddy Angel
6. Sam Majors
7. Bar tender
8. Jill Farrell
9. James T. Pendelton
10. The Cook
11. Polly Temple
12. Jeff Perry
13. Mary Singleton
14. Dr. Herold Hastings
Objects
15. Finger prints on cup
16. Note
17. Book on bear hunting
18. History of lodge
19. Knife
20. After shave spray
21. Revolver
22. Rifle
23. Diary
24. Short Wave Radio
25. Photos
26. Gold
27. Secret Door

Figure 6.22 The objects are added to the layout and the legend.

Notice that only numbers are added to the layout for the objects. Drawing an object that is too small to be seen in a scale drawing is a waste of effort. Usually a number and description in the legend is sufficient.

The level layout is now finished and ready to add to the design document. Only events are not included in the layout at this stage. These can be added if they are needed the same way that the objects were.

Illustrating Environments

The environment illustration is one of the most creative areas of game art creation. Unlike level layouts or storyboards, the environment illustration is not constrained by the need for painstaking accuracy. It is an illustration of the game world designed to give the development team a feeling for the mood and nature of a particular area. This is not to say that there is no need for accuracy in an environment sketch or illustration. It is just to say the need for accuracy is not as high because their purpose is different.

This section will explore the uses and purposes of environment sketches and illustrations in game development. It will also give step-by-step examples for creating an environment sketch and an environment illustration.

What Is an Environment Illustration?

An environment illustration is a detailed picture of an area of the game world. It is usually taken from the same view that the player will see, but it can also be an overview of the world or any other view that communicates how the environment should look. It is in reality a painting of the game world as if the game artist set up an easel and painted the scene.

The size and detail of an environment illustration varies. Some are large and expansive, showing a large area of a game level similar to a panorama. Others are intimate, showing a small view or a single item in the level. Some will have extensive detail, while others have little specific detail but show more of the mood of the area.

Uses and Purposes

Environment sketches and illustrations are used to inspire and give direction to the development team. The game artist will not be able to illustrate every area in a level. It would take hundreds of illustrations to define every area in a game. Rather, the artist's job is to capture the mood and feeling of an area and then let the development team artists expand it to cover the entire level.

Inspiration

The environment illustration is best when it is an inspirational work of art. The more the game artist can capture the feel of an area in the illustration, the better the development team will be able to interpret that feeling throughout the level. This is one of the main reasons that environment illustration is more creative than other game art. Art for inspiration is very different than art for information.

When creating an inspirational piece, the artist must first determine the mood and character of the area that she or he needs to depict. For example, if the game is a cartoon-style platform game, the artist shouldn't try to create a realistic highly detailed illustration. Rather, the illustration should convey the feeling of the finished game. On the other hand, if the game is a horror survival game, the artist should not create the level illustration in a cartoon style.

Finding Inspiration

When creating inspirational work, it is helpful for the artist to be inspired first. Sometimes the most difficult part of drawing is deciding what to draw. This is where devoting some time to a series of thumbnail sketches is helpful. It also helps to spend some time studying other art.

A good way to gain inspiration is to become immersed in the best examples of art available for the type of game being designed. Look at other games in the same genre to see what has been done in the past. If there are any good movies in the genre of the game, view them to see what the Hollywood artists are doing.

Perhaps the best inspiration of all is to look at great art. Look at the masterpieces of the great artists of the past. There is nothing that inspires quite like great art. A little study of art history will pay big dividends to any game artist. A quick trip to a museum is a great way to help the artist begin to put together some ideas for game levels. If there are no museums in the area, spend some time on the Internet or in art history books. Look in Appendix A for some helpful websites for finding examples of great art.

Direction

While inspiration is a major part of an environment illustration, it is not the only purpose. In many areas of a level there will be specific items or scenery that will be needed in the game. Environment illustrations can be used to show the development team a specific area or item. For example, if the game is a futuristic adventure game and the design calls for a special kind of force field around a quest item, it would be much easier to show the field in an illustration than to describe it. With the illustration, the chance of error in creating the force field is greatly reduced.

The game artist will work with the designer to come up with a vision for each area in a game. Using the level layout, the designer and game artist will then identify the areas that will need to be illustrated. Each level will need at least one illustration to set the mood for the level. The other illustrations will be based on the need to give specific information to the development team.

Some levels may have more than one type of area. A level may have a large abandoned warehouse, but inside one area of the warehouse there may be a lush living area for a drug dealer. In situations like that, the game artist will need to create an environment illustration for each unique area in a level.

Some levels may change. There may be weather effects in a racing game, for example, or the level may change appearance depending on the time of day. The game artist should create an illustration for how the level might change so the development team can implement the changes.

Creating an Environment Sketch

Environment sketches are usually black and white drawings of an area in a level. They are used primarily where specific information is needed but color is not. An environment sketch takes much less time to create than a color illustration.

The following example is a sketch of an area in a tropical rain forest. The main character is in a jungle. The location is near a vine-covered statue from an ancient building. The statue will serve as a clue to the player. In order to get the statue to look right, the game artist creates a sketch to show the development team.

The first step in creating the sketch is roughing in the drawing lightly to define the major elements. Draw a few thumbnail sketches, then take the best design and start drawing. Figure 6.23 shows the drawing roughed in. The drawing at this stage is still very loose and free. All that is needed is to define the composition and content of the picture. Notice the composition lines that converge on the character. In environment sketches and illustrations, the artist is freer to use composition techniques than in other types of game art.

Once the framework for the drawing is laid in, the rendering can begin. Figure 6.24 shows the beginning of the rendering. Rendering is the process of adding shading and detail to a picture. In this example, the statue is detailed using a directional stroke to give it the feeling of old weathered stone covered with vines.

Figure 6.23 Rough the composition of the drawing in lightly.

Figure 6.24 Start to render the elements in the drawing.

The two major points of interest in the drawing are the main character and the ancient statue. Define these two elements, then proceed with adding the other parts of the drawing. See Figure 6.25.

Continue to move from section to section of the picture, defining the vegetation and other jungle elements, as shown in Figure 6.26. The lower right half of the picture is beginning to take shape. Some artists prefer to work on the entire picture at once, developing all the areas

Figure 6.25 Define the main character and the statue.

together. In this example, the drawing is developed section by section. Either way works fine as long as the initial construction lines are in and the artist has done a value sketch.

The picture is of a path through the jungle. The jungle is a lush rain forest area so the picture needs to define that in the mind of the viewer. Add detail to the sides of the path so the development team can see the types of plants that are needed in the game. See Figure 6.27.

Figure 6.26 Continue to work on different sections of the picture.

Figure 6.27 Add detail to the path.

The drawing is starting to take shape. Much of the foliage is now in the picture, and it is starting to feel like an enclosed, thickly wooded area. Figure 6.28 shows the picture as it nears completion.

Figure 6.29 shows the near final picture. The development team should be able to get a good idea of how the game will look in this area.

Figure 6.28 Continue to add detail to the background of the picture.

Figure 6.29 The nearly finished drawing.

The last few things to add to the drawing are the distant tree line, some more definition to the mid-ground foliage, and some shading around the character to bring her out more. The sketch is now finished. Figure 6.30 shows the finished sketch.

Figure 6.30 Add the final touches to finish the sketch.

This sketch was created with the player's point of view in mind. The character is in the center of the screen with her back to the viewer. In the next example, we will take a look at creating an environment sketch of a specific location in a game.

For this example, the game takes place in a fantasy environment. The main character lives in a home dug into the side of a hill. The sketch needs to include the character and his home. First, a loose drawing of the home is roughed in along with a couple ovals to indicate where the character will be placed in the drawing. See Figure 6.31.

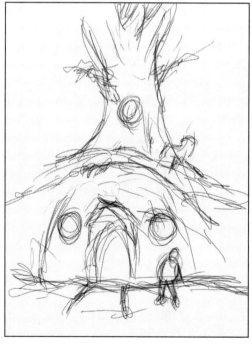

Figure 6.31 Loosely draw the main elements of the picture.

Now a little more detail is added to the character and the entrance of the home, as shown in Figure 6.32.

Now sketch in the rest of the drawing. Make sure that your drawing is still very light. The drawing does not need to be exact. These initial lines are used to guide the later shading lines. See Figure 6.33.

At this point the drawing is still loose. The idea is to get all of the elements of the drawing in place and defined to the point that greater detail can be added over the lighter construction lines. Figure 6.34 is a close-up view of the main character. He is drawn in over the top of the lighter construction lines.

Figure 6.35 shows a better view of how the drawing should look at this stage. The earlier pictures were printed darker than the drawing so the lines would be visible in the printed book. The drawing is now in the detail and shading stage. Notice that the window behind the main character is drawn over the original sketch.

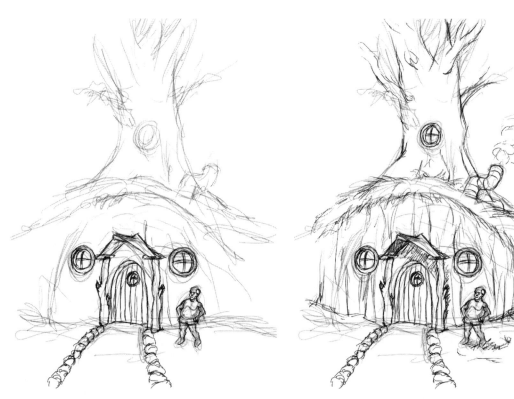

Figure 6.32 Define some of the character and the entrance to the home.

Figure 6.33 Continue to develop the rest of the drawing.

Figure 6.34 Draw the main character over the top of the construction lines.

Figure 6.35 Continue to define the elements surrounding the character.

The next area of importance in the picture will be the entrance to the home, as shown in Figure 6.36.

The next stage of the drawing shows further work on the lower area of the house. The pathway is also drawn. See Figure 6.37.

Figure 6.36 Draw and shade the area of the doorway.

Figure 6.37 Further work is done on the lower area of the house.

Now the upper part of the main character's home is drawn in, as shown in Figure 6.38.

Finish the picture by adding a little more shading and a few finishing touches, as shown in Figure 6.39.

Try drawing a few environment sketches of your own. See if you can convey some emotion in the sketches, like fear or peacefulness.

Figure 6.38 Draw in the upper part of the home.

Figure 6.39 The picture is finished by adding a few final touches.

Summary

This chapter was designed to give you a better understanding of how to draw game art for level designs. It covered creating level layouts and drawing environment sketches. The concepts covered under these two areas were as follows:

- Description of level layouts
- How level layouts are used
- Using layouts as templates
- Using layouts to create asset lists
- Using layouts to direct the game story
- Using layouts to place characters and objects
- Using layouts to place events
- Using layouts to define paths
- Information included in a level layout
- Environment sketches
- Environment illustrations
- How environment sketches are used in game development
- Why environment sketches have more design freedom than other concept art
- How environment sketches give direction and inspiration to the development team

You should now be familiar with the basic structures of level layouts, including how they are created and used in game designs. You should also know how to communicate your ideas for level design to the development team through layouts and level sketches.

Questions

1. What is a level layout?
2. Is artistic composition important in level layouts?
3. Is clarity and accuracy important in level layouts?
4. How should elements in a level layout be placed?
5. Level layouts need not be detailed drawings. (True or False)
6. What is the most common use of a level layout?
7. Should the level layout be accurate enough that the development team can use it for a template when creating the game world?
8. Creating game assets is not a major cost factor in game development. (True or False)

9. What makes a great tool for coming up with an asset list?

10. Why are environment sketches more creative than other concept art?

11. Does mood play a role in an environment sketch?

12. What are some good sources of inspiration for creating environment sketches?

13. Besides inspiration, what else are environment sketches used for?

14. Should every level of a game have environment sketches?

15. Why might an artist create more than one environment sketch of the same area?

Answers

1. A scale drawing of a level used as a guide by the development team to create a level in a game

2. No

3. Yes

4. To create a fun experience for the player.

5. False

6. To convey the level design to the development team

7. Yes

8. False

9. Level layouts

10. Not as much need for accuracy

11. Yes

12. Other games, movies, great works of art

13. Show details of objects or areas that the design team wants to communicate to the development team

14. Yes

15. The level may change during the game

Discussion Questions

1. Why are level layouts important?

2. Why is it important to understand the number of assets needed in a game?

3. How can a designer use a level layout to set up a story?

4. How are environment illustrations used in game development?

5. What are some good ways for artists to get inspiration?

Exercises

1. Create a level layout for a side-view platform game. Make the level fun by adding several unique game elements for the player to navigate.

2. Create a level layout for a racing game. Make the course interesting by adding several jumps and other terrain features.

3. Create an environment sketch of a high seas adventure game onboard a pirate ship. Show the deck of the ship and one or more pirate characters.

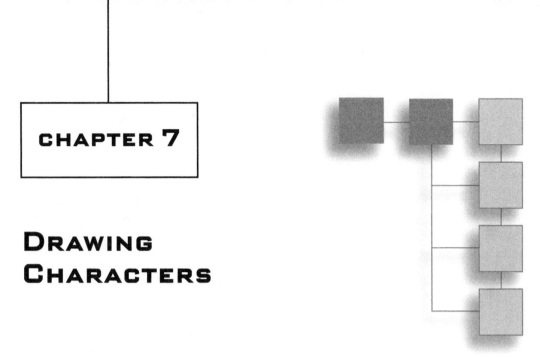

CHAPTER 7

DRAWING CHARACTERS

Creating good game characters is one of the most satisfying and fun aspects of game art. Like the actors and actresses in a motion picture, they are the focus of attention. They are the performers on the stage of the game. Often the player is connected to the game through the game characters. Thus, creating good character art is very important.

This chapter will deal with character sketches and character development. It will also cover basic drawing skills as they relate to character creation.

This chapter will cover the following topics:

- Defining game characters
- Types of game characters
- Getting ideas for characters
- Drawing characters
- Adding character to characters

Game Characters

With the possible exception of some puzzle games, almost every game has characters. A game character is an intelligent person, creature, or machine in a game. Some game characters are beautiful; some are ugly. Some are realistic while others are very simple. There is almost as much variety in game characters as imagination will permit.

Game characters include all intelligent people or creatures in a game. Intelligent means that the character is either controlled by the player or by the game software. The specific software that controls characters in games is called *artificial intelligence*, or AI for short. AI in games is becoming increasingly complex to the point that the player can interact with AI-controlled characters as if they were real.

When game characters first started appearing in games, they were only vague representations of people or creatures. There isn't a lot that an artist can do when the game character is only 16 pixels high. Advances in technology have led to an increase in character size and complexity.

Characters in games are becoming more and more lifelike to the point that they don't just run around and shoot things; they can also have emotion. An angry character will not just attack with sword drawn; he will also have facial expressions and body language to emphasize the attack. Characters in games can have a full range of emotions. This increase in sophistication has increased the demands on designers and game artists to develop interesting and engaging characters.

Types of Game Characters

Games have many different types of characters. The following is a list of categories that game characters can be broken into:

- Player characters
- Nonplayer characters
- Enemies

Each type of character can be further broken down into subtypes. Player characters can be characters controlled by a single player, or in the case of a multiplayer game, characters are controlled by other players. Nonplayer characters or NPCs for short, can be allies, facilitators, or decoration. Enemies can be rivals, aggressive, passive, or traitorous. This breakdown is only one of many ways to categorize characters within a game.

Player Characters

A player character is a character that is controlled by a player. In many games there is only one player character—the one being controlled by the player. Some games, like real-time strategy or team sports games, have the player control multiple characters at once.

The amount of control the player has over a character will depend on the type of game being played. For example, a fighting game will give the player a lot of control over the character. The player will be able to control the movement and actions of the character in detail. Adventure games are similar in that the player will be able to control the character's actions to navigate through the world. Other games, like real-time strategy games, give the player control over position and the character intelligently acts upon the environment and game events.

Multiplayer games have several player-controlled characters in a single game. Some of these games are made up entirely of player-controlled characters. A multiplayer game may have hundreds of player-controlled characters. Many multiplayer games allow the players to customize their characters, some going so far as to include a character editor with the game.

Nonplayer Characters

Technically, any character that is not a player-controlled character is a nonplayer character; however, it is useful to consider enemies a separate group. Enemies are distinct in that players have to react very differently to them than they do to other characters in the game. We will talk about enemies later.

NPCs are usually not overtly hostile to the player. They may be indifferent or have very limited reaction to the player, but they are not generally hostile unless provoked. Of course, if an NPC is provoked, it then can become an enemy rather than an NPC. Likewise, if the player pacifies an enemy, it might change roles as well and become an NPC.

Some games are filled with NPCs. Team sports games, for example, have NPCs that play the role of teammates, cheerleaders, spectators, announcers, and so forth. While they might not necessarily try to kill the player character, the opposing team is better classified as an enemy because their goal is to defeat the player.

Probably the best examples of NPCs are in adventure games. In an adventure game the player interacts with several NPCs on many different levels. Some of the characters in the game may provide information or items to the player. Others may be indifferent yet help in their own way, such as a store clerk or other type of merchant. Some characters may be nothing but decorative, giving no useful information and acting only as a distraction.

In some games, the NPCs change roles depending on the actions of the player. For example, an indifferent merchant may change to an ally if the player completes a quest or helps solve a problem. He may also become an enemy if the player tries to steal something from his shop.

When designing characters, the concept artist needs to understand what the character's role is and create a character that fits that role. A sleazy police informant should not wear a three-piece suit. A military guard should not be slight of build. An opposing linebacker should not be obese. The character needs to fit the role.

Enemies

Enemies are all non-player-controlled characters that try to keep the player from winning the game. The opposing team in a sports game is an enemy. The evil creatures in a horror game are enemies. The other drivers in a racing game are enemies. The vicious alien trying to kill the player in a first-person shooter is an enemy.

In some games enemies are very intelligent and cunning, whereas in others they may just be aggressive. In a football game the opposing team may be very good at play calling and disguising play coverage. In a shooter the enemies may be very good at ganging up on the player. In a fighting game the opponent may have several combo moves. Each of these is designed to challenge the player.

In designing enemies the look of the character is often as important as what the character does in the game. The enemy should be intimidating to the player, causing the player to feel a sense of accomplishment when he defeats the enemy. Sometimes the intimidation is from an imposing physical appearance. Other times the intimidation is subtler, like in a quiz game where the opponent needs to appear intelligent.

Drawing Characters

Drawing characters is maybe one of the most difficult tasks a game artist will have to deal with. The problem is compounded when the character is human. The issue with human characters is that everybody is familiar with the human form. If the artist moves a branch on a tree, for example, few people will notice; however, most people will recognize a person's eye having moved a fraction of an inch. Creating great human characters requires that the artist become very good at drawing the human figure.

Start with the Head

We will begin with the head. Game characters have all shapes and sizes of heads, from cartoon styles to very realistic. Using sound drawing principles will improve the design of the character no matter what the style might be.

Let's start with a simple cartoon-style head and then move on to a more realistic approach. Begin with a circle, as shown in Figure 7.1.

The circle now needs to be made into something that has dimension. It needs to become a 3-dimensional object. Drawing some additional lines around the circle to indicate a sphere, as shown in Figure 7.2, does this.

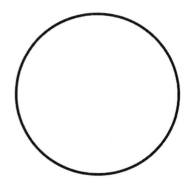

Figure 7.1 Begin drawing the head by drawing a circle.

In the above example the lines carry through the circle, but the lines on the front of the circle are bolder than the lines on the back to help avoid confusion. The new lines not only give the sphere dimension, they also help with the placement of features. These lines are called construction lines. They are usually drawn very lightly. Figure 7.3 is a guide that you can copy from the book to practice drawing cartoon heads.

Use the lines on the sphere as a guide to place the features of the face. Where the two lines cross on the front of the sphere is where the character's nose is placed. Place the eyes along the horizontal line and the mouth and nose along the vertical line. Place the ears behind the other vertical line along the side of the face, as shown in Figure 7.4.

Once you have a good idea of where the features should go, then go ahead and draw the head in bolder. (See Figure 7.5.) Using this method will help to keep the features where they belong and give the face a feeling of dimensionality.

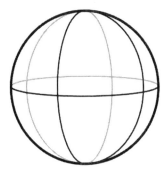

Figure 7.2 Draw some longitudinal and latitudinal lines around the circle.

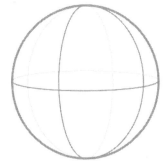

Figure 7.3 Use this picture to copy and practice drawing cartoon heads.

Figure 7.4 Lightly draw the features using the construction lines as guides.

Figure 7.5 Draw the character's head over the construction lines.

The sphere can be drawn with the construction lines rotated in any direction. (See Figure 7.6.) Try drawing the sphere facing up, down, and sideways. Be creative and see what you can come up with.

Figure 7.6 Rotate the sphere to have characters look in different directions.

Drawing Realistic Heads

Drawing a sphere is fine for a cartoon head, but realistic human heads are not perfect spheres. The human has a unique shape that can only loosely be defined by simple geometric shapes. The simple geometric shapes used to construct the human head should be thought of as loose guidelines, not as strict guides.

To draw the construction lines for the human head, start with the cartoon sphere and draw in a jawbone line. Figure 7.7 shows the construction lines for guides in drawing a realistic human head.

Below is a guideline that you can copy and use to practice drawing a head. Do several drawings. Try to do both a male and a female head. (See Figure 7.8.)

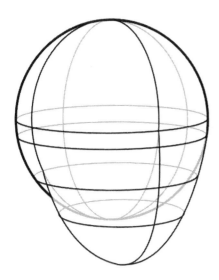

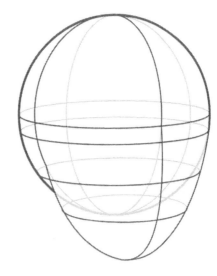

Figure 7.7 Add a jaw line to the cartoon sphere.

Figure 7.8 Use this template to draw several heads as practice.

Figure 7.9 shows the head construction from the front and the side.

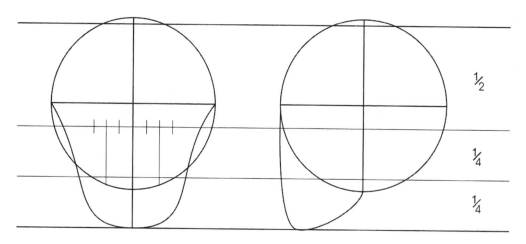

Figure 7.9 Notice the difference between the side view and the front view.

Now how does this simple geometric shape compare to the actual shape of the human head? In Figure 7.10, the geometric shape is superimposed over a drawing of a head.

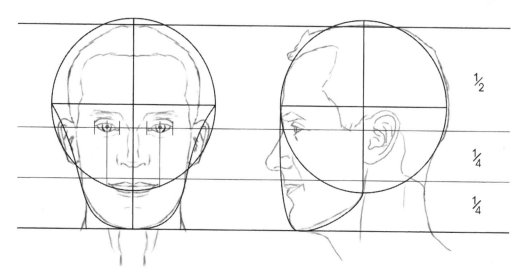

Figure 7.10 Compare the simple geometric shape with an actual head.

There are several things to notice when comparing the shape with the actual head.

- The head is narrower from the front than the sphere.
- The sphere comes above the head slightly.
- The centerline of the sphere is just above the eyebrows.
- The nose protrudes out from the line for the jaw.
- The ear is behind the centerline from the side.
- The top of the ear is level with the eyebrows.
- The eyes are about one eye width apart.
- The mouth follows the sphere line from the front view.
- The nose is about one eye width at the nostrils.
- The edges of the mouth line up closely to the center of the eyes.
- The eyes are almost exactly halfway from the top of the head to the chin.

Of course, this example is only one person. Some people will have large chins while others will have receding chins. Some will have high foreheads while others will have low foreheads. Some people have very round faces while others are oval. Using the simple construction lines will enable you to define the differences.

Now let's take a look at creating a finished drawing of a game character. In Figure 7.11 the head is defined lightly with the construction lines. In addition, the character's helm and armor are also lightly defined.

Figure 7.11 Draw the character's head over the construction lines.

The beginning lines are not exact, but they do give a basis for adding the features of the face. Figure 7.12 shows the features added to the drawing along with other detail on the helm and the armor.

Once the drawing is well defined, it is time to start the rendering process. I usually start with the eyes for two reasons. First, the eyes are usually the focus of interest in a picture of a character. Second, the eyes usually have a great deal of contrast between dark and light. When doing a portrait, it is important to establish the amount of contrast in the picture as a guide for the rest of the drawing. Figure 7.13 shows the beginning of the rendering process.

After the eyes, the next area I focus on is the face. Here I have to be very careful to make sure every element is where it should be. The nose is particularly important to get right because it is the anchor for the rest of the features. Sometimes artists struggle with the nose because it generally blends with the face. Study the nose carefully and use delicate differences in light and shade to define its shape.

Figure 7.12 Draw character's facial features and add detail to the rest of the drawing.

Figure 7.13 The eyes help to establish the amount of contrast in the drawing.

Most of the shadow of the mouth is under the upper lip. The lips are also slightly darker in color than the surrounding face unless, of course, the person is using lipstick; then the lips might be much darker than the surrounding face. Whether the person has colored lips or not, the upper lip is almost always darker than the lower lip when the subject is lit from above. Figure 7.14 shows the portrait with the features drawn.

After the facial features are drawn, the rest of the face is completed, including the hair. The easiest way to think of drawing hair is to start from the darker areas and draw the hair one strand at a time moving from the dark to the light. As you move your pencil, apply less and less pressure. A good example of this technique is the hair right behind the ear, as shown in Figure 7.15. You will need to keep a pencil sharpener handy to draw the hair in this way.

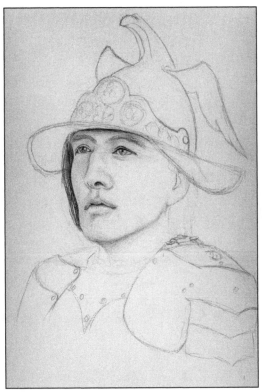

Figure 7.14 Carefully draw the facial features.

Figure 7.15 Draw the hair as single pencil strokes.

Next to the face, the helmet is the most important element of the picture. In some places the helmet is shiny and in others it is not. If you want something to look shiny, you have to draw the reflection. (See Figure 7.16.)

Drawing in the armor completes the drawing. Notice that as the drawing proceeds from the face outward, the armor becomes less and less detailed. This helps to bring the focus of the drawing to the character's face. At this point I take a final look at the drawing to make any changes that are needed. Figure 7.17 shows the finished drawing.

Not all drawings for game characters need to be finished portraits. A lot will depend on the importance of the character. If the character is a main character, a detailed drawing is always advisable.

Figure 7.16 Some parts of the helmet are shiny.

Figure 7.17 The armor becomes less detailed with distance from the character's face.

Drawing the Full Figure

Drawing the figure is similar to drawing the head, except where the head is pretty much a ball with features added, the figure is a flexible form with extreme movement possibilities. When drawing the figure, the artist needs to interpret the dynamics of the range of motion within the character's pose. The artist also needs to take into account things like balance, distribution of weight, action, and proportions. This all sounds complex, but it can be simplified in a similar way as drawing the head. If you can draw a stick figure, you can begin to draw characters. Figure 7.18 shows a typical stick figure. Next to him is the figure we will use to create characters.

The main difference for the new stick figure is that it includes an oval for the ribcage and a trapezoid for the hips. It is also proportionally correct for the average human character. Figure 7.19 shows the stick figure from the back, front, and side views.

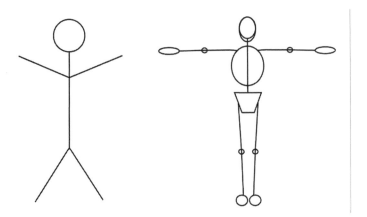

Figure 7.18 The stick figure as he was and as he will become

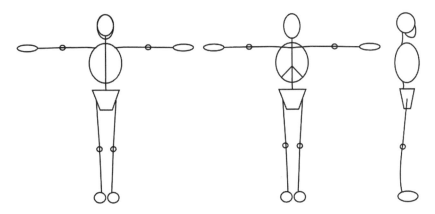

Figure 7.19 The stick figure from the back, front, and side.

In Figure 7.20 the stick figure is overlaid with a drawing of the ideal male proportions. Try drawing a few stick figures to get the proportions right.

Once you get the basics of the stick figure down you can start moving him around to almost any action, like the one shown in Figure 7.21. The stick figure here is high stepping and appears to be moving in an animated way.

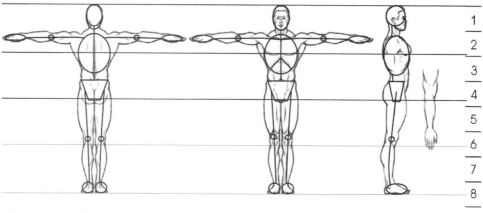

Figure 7.20 The stick figure overlaid with actual human proportions.

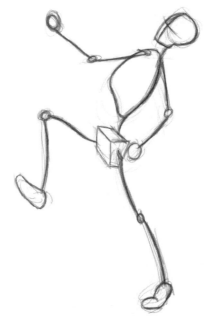

Figure 7.21 The stick figure is easy to animate.

Creating the stick figure in action begins with a simple line called an action line. The action line is the main line of movement of the body. If you can visualize the body moving in space and can define the line of movement from the head along the spine and then through the legs, you will have the action line. Figure 7.22 shows the beginning action line for a stick figure.

Over the top of the action line, the stick figure is loosely sketched in to indicate the position of the torso and the limbs. Notice how the figure follows the action line in Figure 7.23.

Figure 7.22 Start the drawing with a single action line.

Figure 7.23 Sketch the stick figure along the action line.

The action line helps to give the character a feeling of movement. Notice that even though the character's right leg is lifted and pointing toward us, it can still be drawn with the stick figure. Limbs that are pointing toward the viewer are sometimes tricky for beginning artists. The key is to draw the stick figure correctly. Look how that part of the character is drawn in Figure 7.24. To make the figure look correct, you have to think about where the leg is in space and what you would actually see from your point of view. Drawing the body correctly when part or all of it is rotated toward the viewer is called foreshortening.

Figure 7.25 shows the completed stick figure in action. This could be a superhero pose for a super powerful game character. The only thing that remains now is to add some flesh to the sticks, or bones.

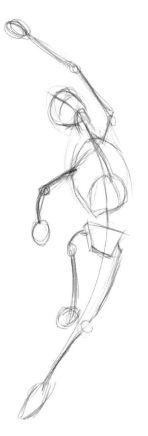

Figure 7.24 Some of the limbs of the body are foreshortened.

Figure 7.25 The finished stick figure should look like a superhero taking flight.

Drawing the Character Sketch

Standing characters should have a distribution of weight between their two legs. One leg can be carrying the majority of the weight, but to look correct, it should be positioned under the character so the weight is balanced over that leg, unless the character is caught in some dynamic action.

Note

In the following example, rather than using pencil and paper, I chose to draw the character digitally in Corel Painter. Painter works great for character designs because the brushes are very similar to actual pencil lines. In Painter I have the ability to change and adjust any part of the character I choose. I can erase and move elements of the character without worrying about the paper surface. I can also undo strokes that I don't like.

The first step in creating a figure is to define the natural position of the body with a few lines that define the relative placement of limbs and balance. Figure 7.26 shows the basic layout of the character. The character is standing in a power pose with his legs separated and his chest forward. Notice that this is not the standard proportion of the stick figures we drew earlier. The character's chest and shoulders are exaggerated to give him a more powerful look.

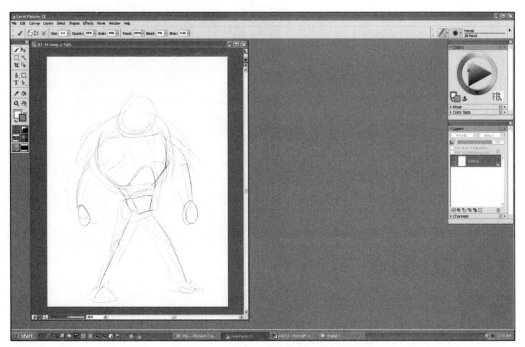

Figure 7.26 Use lines to define body positions and weight distribution.

When drawing a figure, one of the biggest mistakes an artist can make is committing to a specific line too early. It is better to draw multiple lines in an attempt to get a feeling for the figure. Draw the lines lightly and define the forms with pencil strokes. Figure 7.27 shows how the figure starts to emerge out of the many construction lines used in the drawing.

The same loose approach to defining the figure is also used to define the clothing. I am not too worried about getting each line exactly where it belongs. I am more searching for what feels right. Because I am using digital media, I'm not concerned with how dark the lines are. I use a build-up method to define each detail of the figure. (See Figure 7.28.)

Now that I have a good set of construction lines defining my character, it is time to make the fade so they become light enough for construction purposes. I use the Adjust Color feature in Corel Painter in the Effects/Tonal Control menu. Move the value slider to the right to have the picture fade into usable construction lines. You may have to adjust the color more than once to get the desired effects. Figure 7.29 shows the faded construction lines.

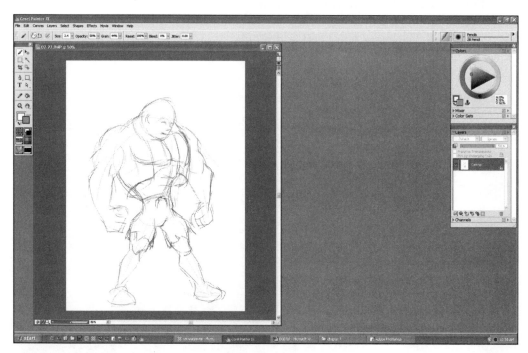

Figure 7.27 Many lines are drawn to define the form of the body.

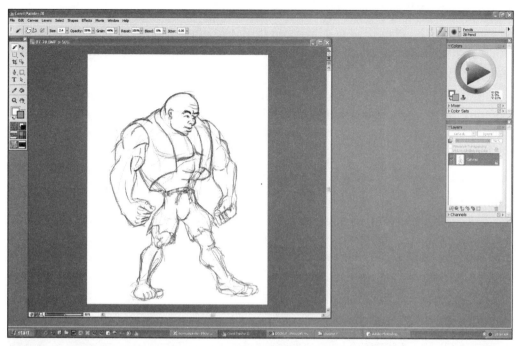

Figure 7.28 Continue to define the character and clothing.

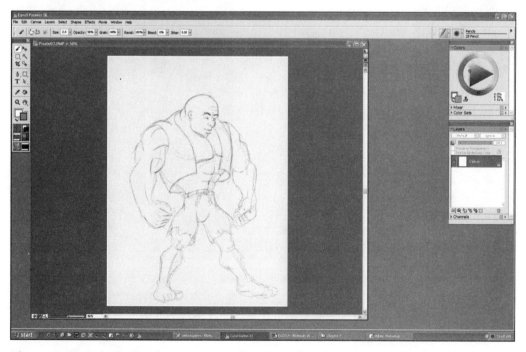

Figure 7.29 Fade the drawing to prepare it for more defined lines later.

When the basic shapes are defined, more definite lines can be used to render the character. Figure 7.30 shows the stronger lines and shades starting to come out of the lighter construction lines. In some places the earlier lines need to be cleaned up to better show the new, more definite lines.

I continue to draw in the cleaner, more defined lines as I work my way down the figure. One nice thing about using digital media is not having to worry about smudging my drawings. I can work on any part of the drawing without worrying about where I place my hand.

Figure 7.31 shows the drawing after the new, cleaner lines are applied.

Using the Eraser feature I clean up the construction lines around the character. I also increase the contrast of the image to get rid of any remaining construction lines that I don't want to appear in the final sketch. Figure 7.32 shows the final results. This sketch is now ready to add color to or to leave black and white depending on the needs of the design.

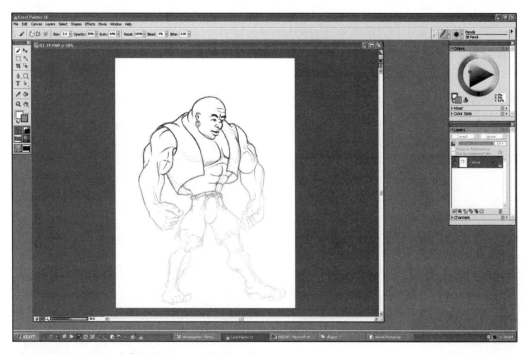

Figure 7.30 More definite lines are added to the drawing.

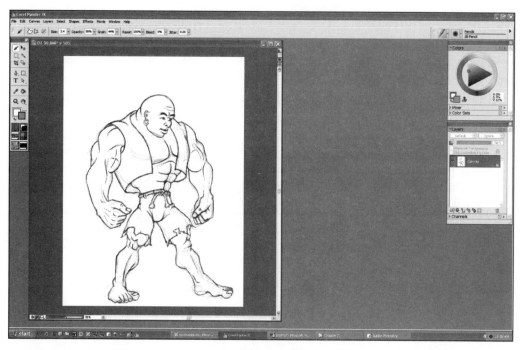

Figure 7.31 The cleaner lines are drawn over the construction lines.

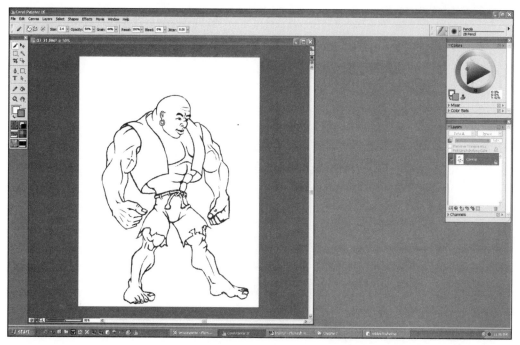

Figure 7.32 The finished character sketch.

Nonhuman Characters

Some characters in games are nonhumans. They may be animals, robots, aliens, imaginary or fantasy creatures, or about anything the designer's imagination can come up with. Drawing these types of characters is both creative and challenging—creative because the artist can use a lot of imagination; challenging because there are less structural guidelines.

Hint

When drawing imaginary characters it is a good practice to base the character on some form of reality. Make sure the joints work. The muscles should move the limbs in the right directions. The character should look like it could move and work in a normal environment with the same gravitational effects as the rest of the characters in the game.

As always the best way to start drawing a character is to do a few thumbnail sketches of the character until there is something that looks good. Choose the best idea and then rough in the idea with light construction lines, as shown in Figure 7.33.

Figure 7.33 Lightly draw the construction lines for the character.

This character is a mage creature from some ancient underground race. He is humanoid in that he walks semierect on two legs. His hand and feet are clawed and his skin is knobby and leathery. His clothing is ceremonial rather than used as covering.

The beginning of the drawing should be free and flowing. Continue to define the creature. Figure 7.34 shows the progress.

The drawing is now beginning to take shape. Define the facial features and continue to work on the cloak and staff. The drawing should look like Figure 7.35.

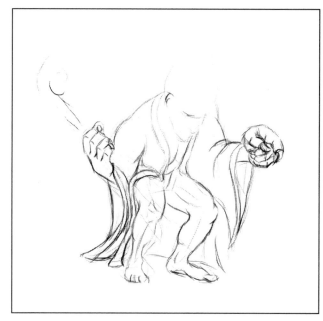

Figure 7.34 Add more definition to the drawing.

Figure 7.35 Add facial features and detail to the staff.

As the drawing becomes more defined, the lines become more deliberate and less free flowing. Figure 7.36 shows the character as he starts to come together as a more solid form. Notice the bumpy skin of the head and the shading of the cloak.

Now that the drawing is well defined in shape and form, the detail and shading can be added. Figure 7.37 shows the finished drawing. Because the construction lines were drawn in lightly there is almost no cleanup necessary at the end of the drawing.

When it comes to imaginary characters there are an infinite variety of possibilities. Sometimes the artist will come up with great ideas for characters by experimental drawing, but the best way to approach the creation of an imaginary creature is to write a brief description of the character before sketching. At the beginning of this exercise there was a written description of the character. This written description helped in creating the character and keeping him in line with the needs of the game.

Figure 7.36 Start refining the forms in the drawing by adding detail and shading.

Figure 7.37 Continue to add detail and shading until the sketch is finished.

Summary

Character creation is one of the most rewarding and challenging jobs of the game artist. It is very rewarding for the artist to see a character that she designed in a game. It is also challenging to come up with characters that enhance the game design.

This chapter was devoted to character creation and drawing. The reader should now be familiar with many aspects of character creation. The topics discussed in this chapter include the following:

- Game characters
- Player characters
- Non-player characters
- Enemies
- Drawing the cartoon head
- Drawing the realistic head
- Drawing the stick figure
- Drawing the stick figure in action
- Exaggerating the figure
- Nonhuman characters

Questions

1. Why is character creation important in game design?
2. Who has the main responsibility for the creation of interesting characters?
3. What are game characters?
4. What is the software that controls characters in games called?
5. A character that is controlled by the player is called what?
6. What do the letters NPC stand for?
7. What makes an NPC an enemy character?
8. Observing people in day-to-day life can serve what purpose for the game artist?
9. What is the basic shape used to start drawing the cartoon head?
10. How do basic geometric shapes help the artist in constructing the head?
11. Why should construction lines be kept free and flowing?
12. What does distribution of weight mean in a character drawing?
13. The few light beginning lines of the position of the limbs and body balanced over the feet defines what?
14. How might exaggerating the size of a character's chest and shoulders affect the look of the character?

15. Should the artist be concerned with proper muscles for movement of a fantasy creature?

Answers

1. Because the characters are the focal point of the game
2. The concept artist
3. All intelligent people or creatures in a game
4. Artificial Intelligence
5. A player character
6. Nonplayer character
7. It is hostile to the player
8. Inspiration for character designs
9. A circle
10. They help to make the head 3-dimensional and they help the artist to place the features correctly
11. So the artist does not commit to a line too early in the drawing process
12. The character should look balanced
13. The natural position of the body
14. A more powerful look
15. Yes

Discussion Questions

1. Why is the study of figure drawing important in character design?
2. How does simplifying figures into simple geometric shapes help the character artist?
3. Why are characters so important in game design?
4. What effect does exaggeration of the head have on a character?
5. What is the future of character design?

Exercises

1. Create a sketch of a main character for a futuristic space game. Make the character pleasant but strong without being overbearing.
2. Create a heroine character for a horror adventure game. Make her appealing without being overtly sexy. Give her a sense of innocence combined with strength.
3. Create an enemy character for a military game that is truly terrifying. He should be the final character in the game and one that will make the player think twice before attacking.

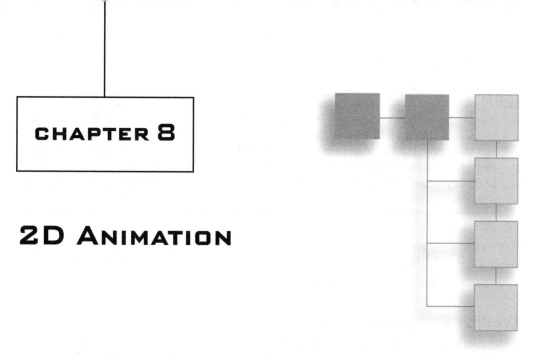

CHAPTER 8

2D ANIMATION

W hen I first started creating games all animation was done in 2D or what is some-times referred to as *cell animation*. The term cell animation comes from the motion picture industry. It refers to how animation was once created on clear plastic pages called cells. These cells were laid over background art and photographed one at a time.

How Does Animation Work?

Animation is the process of taking a series of drawn or rendered pictures and showing them in succession. Each picture has elements that change position from frame to frame. When this happens, the slight differences between pictures give the illusion of movement. This process of showing pictures in rapid succession is the same method used in motion pictures, videos, and TV. A motion picture camera does not record movement; it records a series of still images called *frames*. A frame is a single image in a series of images used in film, video, and animation. If, for example, a motion picture camera is recording a scene from an action car-chase movie, each picture of the cars will be slightly different. The first frame of the car chase might be of the cars in the distance coming toward the camera. Each succeeding frame will have the cars a little closer to the camera. When all the frames are played back in order, the cars will actually appear to move toward the camera.

In motion pictures and TV, the frames are presented so quickly that the normal human eye does not register them as individual frames. In motion pictures, the normal rate of pictures projected on the screen is 24 frames a second, although some will go as high as 70 frames a second. TV and video runs at 30 frames a second. Frame rates in games are not set because often the speed of the computer and complexity of the program determines the frame rate. However, most game developers target 60 frames a second. Games that drop below 30 frames a second are harder to play because the controls will seem sluggish.

Hint

The number of frames a second is very important to the animator. The most common mistake of beginning animators is to make the difference in movement between frames even. They do not take into account that faster movements have greater differences between frames, while slower movements have smaller movements between frames. Movement between frames, however should not be sporadic, causing the animation to have a jerky appearance. Differences in movement rates should be smooth.

Artists use animation to make things move in video games. In 2D animation each movement is drawn by hand. This is a very long and time-consuming process that requires several artists working on a single project.

Creating a Simple 2D Animation

Animated drawings are usually created on semitransparent paper called tracing paper. Tracing paper is available at most art supply stores. The advantage of semitransparent paper is that it allows the artist to see previous drawings and compare them to the present drawing. Some animators will draw on a light box so they can see even more of their previous drawings.

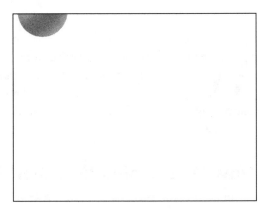

Figure 8.1 Draw the ball at the top of the page.

To do your first animation, start with something simple like a ball. Rather than starting with the top page of a pad of tracing paper, start with the bottom page. Number the pages starting from the back going forward until you have 14 numbered pages. On the first page draw the ball coming down from the top of the left hand side of the page, as shown in Figure 8.1

Next count forward to frame 7 and draw the ball at the bottom middle of the page. Flatten the ball, as shown in Figure 8.2.

Figure 8.2 Draw the ball flattened at the bottom of the page.

Frame seven is called a *key frame.* A key frame is a frame that shows the extent of a single motion. In this case the ball falls from frame 1 to frame 7 where it hits the ground. Hitting the ground is the end of the dropping motion. Frame 1 and frame 7 are special guide frames. They show the extreme points of an action. The frames between 1 and 7 are called *in betweens.* In betweens are usually added after all of the key frames are drawn for a specific sequence.

The flattening of the ball is an exaggeration of what happens in real life. It emphasizes the ball hitting a hard surface. In real life, a ball hitting a hard surface will flatten somewhat depending on the elasticity of the ball. In animation, exaggerating the flattening effect gives the ball a livelier look.

The next key frame is frame 14. In this frame the ball has bounced and is leaving the picture at the upper right-hand side, as shown in Figure 8.3.

Now that all of the key frames are drawn, the in betweens can be added in the remaining frames. First draw frame 4 halfway between frames 1 and 7, as shown in Figure 8.4.

Draw the ball in frame 10 halfway between frame 7 and frame 14, as shown in Figure 8.5.

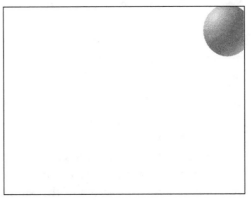

Figure 8.3 The ball is leaving the picture at frame 14.

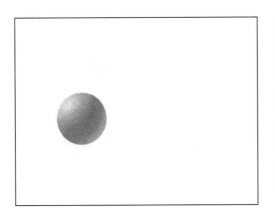

Figure 8.4 The ball is halfway between frames 1 and 7 at frame 4.

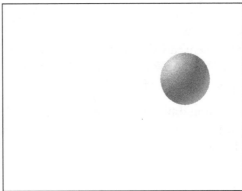

Figure 8.5 The ball in frame 10 is halfway between frame 7 and frame 14.

The remaining in betweens for the animation are frames 2, 3, 5, 6, 8, 9, 11, 12, and 13. For frame 2, put the ball a third of the distance between frames 1 and 4. For frame 3, put the ball two-thirds of the distance between frames 1 and 4. The same procedure will work for frames 5 and 6 between 4 and 7. Frames 8 and 9 will also work the same way between frames 7 and 10. There is one difference in the shape of the ball in frames 8 and 9, however. In frame 8 the ball stretches, as shown in Figure 8.6.

Frame 9 will also have some stretching to it but not as much as frame 8. By the time the ball reaches frame 10, it should be back to its round shape. The stretching exaggeration enhances the elastic feel of the ball.

You will notice that there are three frames between 10 and 14. This is because the ball will slow down as it reaches the height of its bounce. Adding more frames for the same amount of movement will have the effect of slowing the ball because it takes longer for the ball to get from one position to another. We could plot the movement of the ball mathematically, but for a simple movement like this, it will be easier for the animator to place the balls visually.

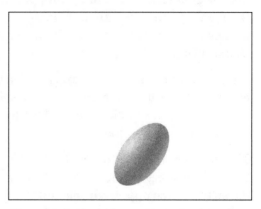

Figure 8.6 The ball stretches as it rebounds from the surface.

First draw a line from the center of the ball in frame 10 to the center of the ball in frame 14. Now place the ball in frame 11 about midway between a quarter and a third of the distance from frame 10 and frame 14. Next place the ball in frame 12 about halfway between one-half and two-thirds of the way along the distance from 10 to 14. For the final ball placement, divide the distance between 12 and 14 in half and place the ball just slightly past half the distance. While this method is not completely accurate, it will give the desired effect of slowing the ball.

You should now have a 14-frame animation of a ball bouncing from left to right across the page. If you flip through the frames in succession, the ball will appear to bounce across the page.

Creating Character Animation

Animating a character is a complex task. There are many things to consider when an animator simulates the movement of a person or creature. In this book we will not have the space to go over every aspect of good character animation. Instead we will focus on the basics. I highly recommend that you experiment with the concepts in this book. You should also study great animated videos or DVDs to see how animators create the illusion of movement. Try going through a video or DVD frame by frame; you will be able to see the differences in each frame.

Comparing Motions

If you are serious about animation, you should take a look at one of my other books, *The Animator's Reference Book*, also by Thomson Course Technology. In this book models were photographed from four different angles while performing common game actions. Using the book, you can compare motions to see how one motion differs from another. The book is also good for comparing how balance is maintained and body movement differs.

Motions vary a great deal. A skip motion is very different from a run motion. A sneak motion is very different from a casual walk. Even walk motions vary depending on the speed. Compare the two photos in Figure 8.7. When the model is carrying a heavy duffle bag, he leans forward. This is to balance the added weight of the duffle bag. The more the bag weighs, the more the model will have to lean forward to balance the weight.

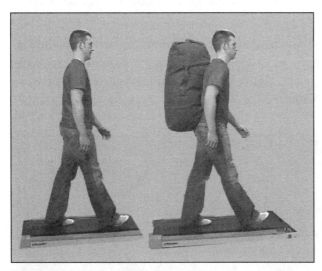

Figure 8.7 The model has to lean forward to balance the weight of the duffle bag.

Weight and Gravity

A common problem with beginning animators is that their characters lack any feeling of weight. Back in Figure 8.7, you can see how carrying the duffle bag changed the way the character walked. Closer study reveals that carrying the duffle bag affected more than just the model's balance. It also affected the effort the model had to make to move. Weight puts more stress on the muscles and joints. This extra stress is evident in the way the model had to move to carry a heavier object.

Even without carrying an object the model still has weight. The sense of weight is most evident in the model's feet, when walking barefoot. When one foot is holding the weight of the model while the other is in the air, the one on the ground will be more compressed and flattened than the one in the air.

Moving weight takes energy. The body supplies this energy in the form of muscle movement. There is really no stress on the arms when casually walking, but there is a lot of stress on the legs. The muscles in the legs will tend to show greater degrees of flexing than the arms.

Observe how weight and gravity affect the human body in motion. Even though some of these effects are subtle, mastering them can bring a huge improvement to animation.

Arcs in Animation

The human body uses a system of bones, joints, and muscles to cause movement. The system always moves in an arc because the joints that anchor the bones to each other act as pivot points.

The concept of arcs has been around for some time in animation. Understanding how to trace these arcs, however, has not been an easy process. Figure 8.8 shows the arc of the head and hand in a typical walk sequence. Notice how the motion of movement between frames in the sequence swings in an arc.

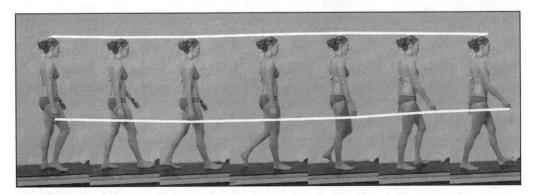

Figure 8.8 All human movement tends to be in arcs.

One way to achieve a believable exaggeration in 2D animation is to exaggerate the arcs of human motion. This type of exaggeration will seem natural to the viewer because it fits with the natural movement of the character.

Internal Animation

The game artist generally will not deal with movement of a character or object across the screen. The game programmer usually does that work, although the game artist may need to show the programmer how far to move a character from frame to frame. What the artist is more likely to deal with is the object's *internal animation*. Internal animation is the movement within a character or object itself rather than the movement across a screen. For example, if a character is walking, the movement of the legs is an internal animation while the progress the character makes across the screen is not. When an artist animates a character walking for a game, he will animate the character walking in place. This is very important because if the artist moves the character, it will make it a lot more difficult for the programmer to move the character in the game.

Character Animation

Many animations in computer games are *cycled animation*. A cycled animation is a looping animation that ends where it starts. For example, most walking and running animation in a game is one full step repeated several times. In the industry it is referred to as a walk or a run cycle. In the following example, we will create a walk cycle for a character.

1. To start this animation we need to bring up an animation window in Corel Painter, as we did in the last example. (See Figure 8.9.)

2. Set the dimensions to 256×256 and the frames to 12. Click Movie and then Okay. Save the movie as "walk," as shown in Figure 8.10.

3. Set the layers to 4 and the color depth to 24 bit, as shown in Figure 8.11.

4. For this animation we will start with a character. I loaded a picture of the character from a drawing that I created earlier. Randy is already in the process of taking a step. (See Figure 8.12.)

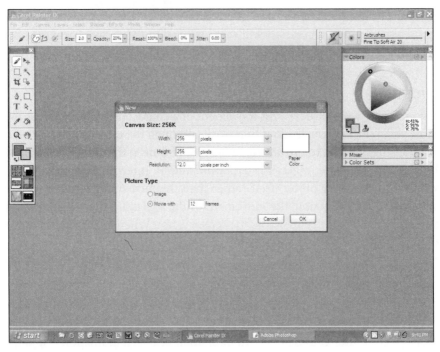

Figure 8.9 The new animation window.

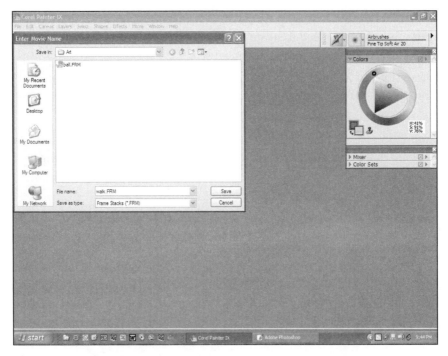

Figure 8.10 The Enter Movie Name menu.

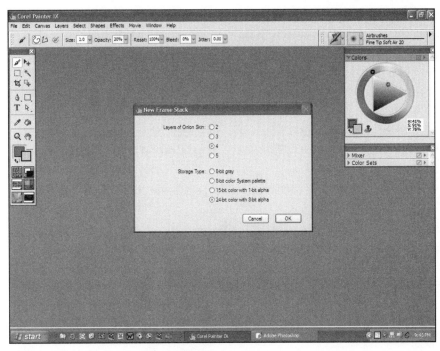

Figure 8.11 The New Frame Stack menu.

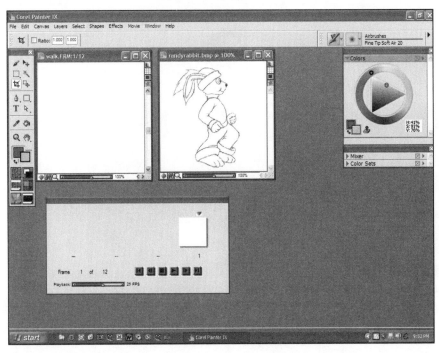

Figure 8.12 A base drawing of the character is loaded as a guide.

5. We now select Randy using the Box Selection tool on the left-hand side of the screen. Drag the box selection around Randy, as shown in Figure 8.13.

6. Once the character is selected, it is an easy process to click on the selected character and drag him over to the animation window. He is now a floating object and can be positioned anywhere on the page. Place him in the middle of the page, as shown in Figure 8.14

7. It is easier to draw an animation if it is larger on screen. At the bottom of the animation window there is a blue bar. This is the magnification control. Slide the bar to the right until it is set to 200%.

8. Now grab the lower right-hand corner and enlarge the window to hold the animation.

9. Use the animation controls to increment the frame forward one frame. The drawing of Randy is now flattened onto the first frame. We will want to change Randy for the second frame, so the floating drawing needs to be deleted. Select Delete Layer from the Layers menu, as shown in Figure 8.15.

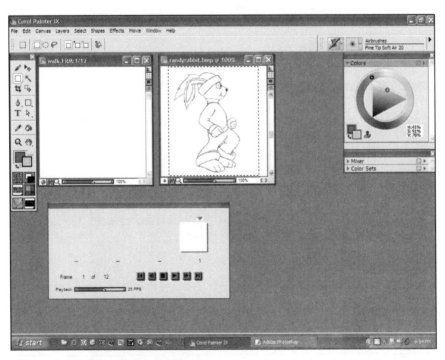

Figure 8.13 Select the character.

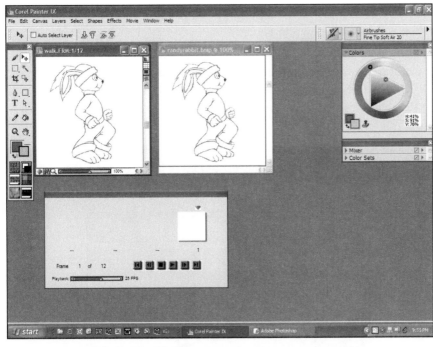

Figure 8.14 The selected character is moved to the animation window.

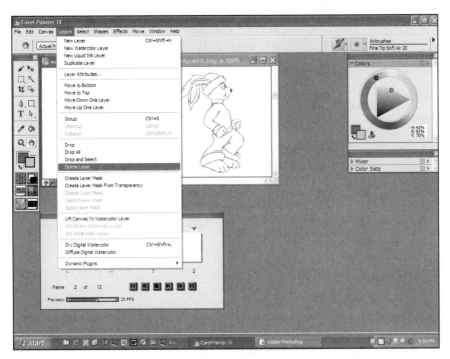

Figure 8.15 Delete the floating layer from frame 2.

10. Next, turn on the tracing paper feature located in the upper right-hand corner of the animation window, as shown in Figure 8.16

11. Now we can see the first drawing through the second frame so that we can use it as a guide for drawing the second frame of the animation. We draw the second frame with Randy's feet and hands moved to a new position. Notice that we also are raising the character slightly in this frame to give him a bounce as he walks. (See Figure 8.17.)

12. Continue to draw new frames of the animation of Randy's walk using the drawings below it as a guide to each drawing, as shown in Figure 8.18.

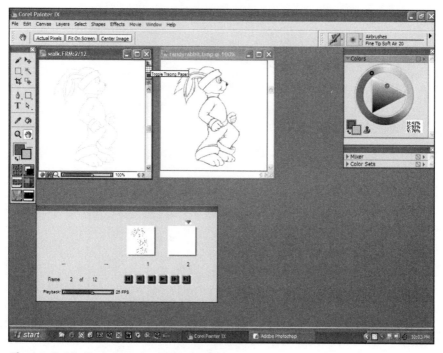

Figure 8.16 Turn on tracing paper.

Figure 8.17 Frame 2 of the animation is drawn.

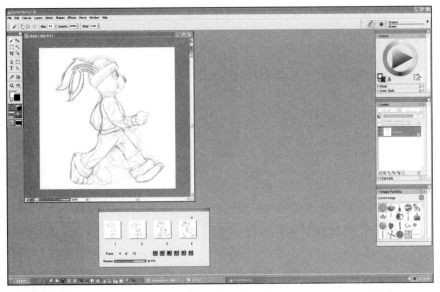

Figure 8.18 Frames 1 through 4 of the animation sequence.

Hint

One of the biggest challenges of animation is timing. In a walk cycle the rate of movement is fairly constant, meaning that the act of walking generally does not have uneven movement. In most cases the animator can divide the distance of movement between each frame evenly. In a 12-frame animation, frames 1 and 7 will look much the same with the only exception being that the left and right sides of the character are reversed. (See Figure 8.19.)

Figure 8.19 Frame 1 and frame 7.

The same thing will be true for frame 2 and 8; frame 3 and 9; frame 4 and 10; frame 5 and 11; and finally frame 6 and 12. If the artist does a good job with the first half of the walk cycle, the second half becomes easier because the first half can be used as a template. Look at Figure 8.20 to see the similarities between frames.

13. Continue drawing each frame. Once you have reached the last frame and have compared each frame as in Figure 8.19, review the motion by incrementing through the animation 1 through 12. Be careful to only go to 12. Corel Painter will automatically add unwanted frames if you increment beyond 12. (See Figure 8.21.)

14. Press the Play button. The animation will run fast, but you will be able to see your work. (See Figure 8.22.) You can slow the animation by adjusting the frame slider on the Animation menu.

Figure 8.20 Similarity between frames of animation.

Figure 8.21 Frame 12 of the animation sequence.

Figure 8.22 Playing the animation.

Summary

In this chapter we looked a 2D animation. The following concepts were covered.

- Defining animation
- Drawing animation
- Exaggeration in animation
- Weight and balance in animation
- Animation arcs
- Animation cycles
- Similarities between frames in a walk animation
- How to create a walk cycle

You should have a beginning understanding of creating 2D animation on paper and with Corel Painter.

This book has covered many aspects of drawing for games. Hopefully it has given you a glimpse into the world of game art and a beginning in understanding how drawing is used in game production. Good drawing skill is important, and as you continue your studies in game art, remember to spend a good amount of your time drawing. Good luck in your efforts.

Questions

1. What frame rate do most game developers target for their games?
2. Why is it not a good idea to have a frame rate below 30 frames a second?
3. Do games have a standard frame rate?
4. Will increasing the distance of movement between frames make an object appear to move faster or slower?
5. What causes jerky animation?
6. The joints and muscles cause the body to move in what?
7. Does carrying weight cause the body to change during movement?
8. Are artists primarily responsible for moving objects and characters from place to place in a computer game?
9. When energy is transferred by an object hitting another object, does it cause the objects to speed up or slow down?
10. Should beginning animators study animated videos and DVDs by great animators?
11. Are programmers generally responsible for internal animation?
12. Will animating a character in place help the programmer to place characters in a game?
13. What are looping animations called?
14. Are cycled animations used very often in computer games?
15. Which frames are more likely to be similar in a 12-frame walk cycle: 1, 10, or 7?

Answers

1. 60 frames a second
2. It causes the controls to be sluggish
3. No
4. Faster
5. Sporadic changes on movement between frames

6. Arcs

7. Yes

8. No, programmers are more likely to deal with movement on screen

9. Slow down

10. Yes, it will help them to see how animators achieve good movement in their characters

11. No, artists usually deal with internal movement

12. Yes

13. Cycled animation

14. Yes

15. Frames 1 and 7 are most similar

Discussion Questions

1. How do games and other media make characters appear to move with a series of static pictures?

2. Why is timing important in animation?

3. Why is animation a time-consuming process?

4. Explain why it is important for the game artist to not move an animated character onscreen when doing internal animation?

5. Why is it important to keep animations smooth?

Exercises

1. Create a simple animation by creating an object like a plane or car and moving it across the screen.

2. Create a walk cycle animation of a character you created.

3. Create a jump animation of a character you created.

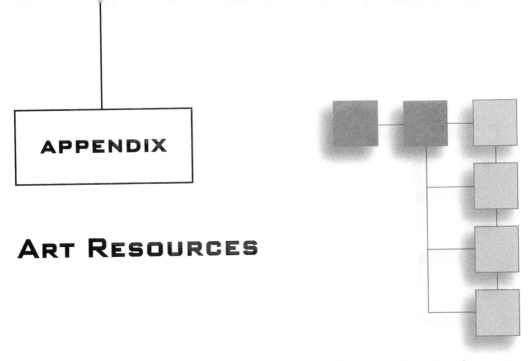

APPENDIX

ART RESOURCES

An artist often spends as much time looking for reference and learning about art as he does drawing. This appendix contains some resources that you might find useful as you develop your skills as a game artist.

Art Instruction

www2.evansville.edu/studiochalkboard/draw.html

http://cyberartlearning.com

www.nms2.com

www.makart.com/resources/artclass

www2.evansville.edu/drawinglab

Figure Drawing Resources

Les Pardew and Ross Wolfley. *The Animator's Reference Book*. Thomson Course PTR: Boston, MA, 2004.

Paul Gonzales III (photographer), Wes Hartman (photographer), and Paula Kilpatrick (photographer). *Posefile Supersize #2 (Posefile Reference Action Pose Collection)*. Antarctic Press: San Antonio, TX, 2004.

E.A. Ruby. *The Human Figure: A Photographic Reference for Artists*. John Wiley & Sons: New York, NY, 1974.

Thomas Easley and Mark Smith (photographer). *The Figure in Motion*. Watson Guptill: New York, NY, 1986.

In addition, you may want to take a look at the following websites:

www.3d.sk

www.virtualpose.net

www.modelalisa.com

INDEX

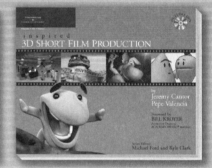

Bring your ideas to life!

Today's animation audience expects more than a nice picture to believe in a character. Now you can develop the skills and techniques you need to create characters that will draw your audience into the world you've created.

Thomson Course Technology is proud to be the official publisher for Softimage Co.

Maya 6 Revealed
ISBN: 1-59200-365-6 ■ $24.99

Get ready to explore all that Maya 6 has to offer! Giving you a firm foundation, *Maya® 6 Revealed* allows you to master concepts on both a technical and artistic level. Begin by examining the concept behind each task—the goal and the necessary features that are involved. Then go in-depth with the objective of your task as you study examples and learn the steps necessary to complete it. Working your way through comprehensive, step-by-step lessons, you'll develop the confidence you need to create amazing graphics using Maya 6.

Experience XSI 4
ISBN: 1-59200-210-2 ■ $49.99

Take an exclusive look into how the design process of characters for motion pictures has changed through the application of XSI. Develop the skills you need to create a detailed animated character that can then be composited into a live action scene using the XSI compositor. Author Aaron Sims includes his own incredible characters to demonstrate the techniques applied in their creation and co-author Michael Isner of Softimage discusses the groundbreaking technology and powerful tool set that XSI delivers.

Inspired 3D Short Film Production
ISBN: 1-59200-117-3 ■ $59.99

Digital 3D Design
ISBN: 1-59200-391-5 ■ $24.99

Hollywood 2D Digital Animation:
The New Flash Production Revolution
ISBN: 1-59200-170-X ■ $39.99

Adobe Photoshop for VFX Artists
ISBN: 1-59200-487-3 ■ $39.99

Creating 3D Effects for Film, TV, and Games
ISBN: 1-59200-589-6 ■ $49.99

Gamedev.net

The most comprehensive game development resource

- The latest news in game development
- The most active forums and chatrooms anywhere, with insights and tips from experienced game developers
- Links to thousands of additional game development resources
- Thorough book and product reviews
- Over 1,000 game development articles!
  Game design
  Graphics
  DirectX
  OpenGL
  AI
  Art
  Music
  Physics
  Source Code
  Sound
  Assembly
  And More!

 Gamedev.net